Organizational Change

Peter Floyd

- ■ Fast track route to managing organizational change

- ■ Covers the key areas of change, from initiating change through to making it happen, including managing the pitfalls and issues that arise in any change initiative and then sustaining the change so it sticks

- ■ Examples and lessons from some of the world's most successful businesses, including Sony, Daimler-Chrysler and General Electric, and ideas from the smartest thinkers, including Peter Senge, Eddie Obeng, Jeannie Daniel Duck, Michael Beer, Jay Lorsch, Julia Balogun and Veronica Hope-Hailey

- ■ Includes a glossary of key concepts and a comprehensive resources guide

ORGANIZATIONS

07.06

>>EXPRESS EXEC.COM<<
essential management thinking at your fingertips

Copyright © Capstone Publishing 2002

The right of Peter Floyd to be identified as the author of this work has been asserted in accordance with the Copyright, Designs and Patents Act 1988

First published 2002 by
Capstone Publishing (a Wiley company)
8 Newtec Place
Magdalen Road
Oxford OX4 1RE
United Kingdom
http://www.capstoneideas.com

CIP catalogue records for this book are available from the British Library and the US Library of Congress

ISBN 1-84112-197-5

Printed and bound by CPI Antony Rowe, Eastbourne

Contents

Introduction to ExpressExec

ExpressExec is 3 million words of the latest management thinking compiled into 10 modules. Each module contains 10 individual titles forming a comprehensive resource of current business practice written by leading practitioners in their field. From brand management to balanced scorecard, ExpressExec enables you to grasp the key concepts behind each subject and implement the theory immediately. Each of the 100 titles is available in print and electronic formats.

Through the ExpressExec.com Website you will discover that you can access the complete resource in a number of ways:

» printed books or e-books;
» e-content – PDF or XML (for licensed syndication) adding value to an intranet or Internet site;
» a corporate e-learning/knowledge management solution providing a cost-effective platform for developing skills and sharing knowledge within an organization;
» bespoke delivery – tailored solutions to solve your need.

Why not visit www.expressexec.com and register for free key management briefings, a monthly newsletter and interactive skills checklists. Share your ideas about ExpressExec and your thoughts about business today.

Please contact elound@wiley-capstone.co.uk for more information.

Introduction

» The environments that organizations find themselves in are changing very quickly.
» Change programs have had a poor track record to date.
» There is an increasing need for organizational change (OC), which addresses this issue.
» Change is both initiated and restrained by people.

"I'm all for progress; it's change I don't like."

Mark Twain

Mark Twain neatly sums up the dilemma facing organizations and their employees as we move into the twenty-first century. Unprecedented levels of turbulence and change mean that organizations are under constant pressure to respond and adapt.

How they handle these changes and move forward will determine either their continued success or their likely demise.

Experience has shown that the first step, the initiation of change, is the easy one. The real challenge and the major source of difficulty is the implementation of changes, turning ideas and plans into reality.

Organizational change (OC) is about this whole process, from defining the change, through to making it happen. Change programs to date have a relatively poor track record, and many change initiatives are either halted or fail to achieve their expected results. It is estimated that only 30% of programs lead to a successful outcome. However, there are *huge* benefits and gains for organizations that can learn to manage change effectively. OC, therefore, is becoming one of the most important fields in management today. In spite of this, it is one of the least well-defined and understood subjects. It is a complex area.

The complicated nature of change means that it is inherently a difficult process to manage. There are a vast number and range of influences involved in OC, from customer needs through to employee needs and shareholder needs. Achieving a win-win situation for all the interested parties is the art of OC.

The material contained in this book demonstrates that, to be successful, organizations must engage as wide a group as possible in a debate about options and solutions. In fact, the label "OC" de-personalizes the real issue, that of human change. The solutions to complex change issues lie at the heart of an organization: its people. This includes everyone involved in a change process, from the employees with great ideas, through executives managing large change programs, to employees who are themselves having to undergo change.

When considering OC, our focus must be on people and on the inherent issues of awareness, ownership, involvement, skills, and commitment.

This book aims to provide a starting point for individuals striving to initiate, plan, and implement change in their organization. It discusses the development of OC and defines a broad pragmatic framework for managing change.

In order to illustrate best practice, the book provides a number of topical case studies and looks at the leading ideas in the field, supplying examples of the particular issues raised.

It includes practical advice and tools. In particular, Chapter 10 outlines a 10 step process to implementing OC effectively.

May your future changes be successful ones!

Definition of Terms

» There are many possible models for an organization, ranging from the mechanistic to the humanistic.
» OC involves the whole process from strategy formulation through to strategy implementation.
» OC is a rather ambiguous and poorly understood concept.
» There are many suggested definitions for OC.
» At the highest level these are well-defined and understood.
» The most common view of OC is that it relates to the organizational and human factors of change.
» Another view is to see OC as the who, why, what, and how of change in organizations.
» There are a number of other related terms, such as strategy, change agent etc.

"There is no more delicate matter to take in hand, nor more dangerous to conduct, nor more doubtful in its success, than to be a leader in the introduction of changes. For he who innovates will have for enemies all those who are well off under the old order of things, and only lukewarm supporters in those who might be better off under the new."

N. Machiavelli

Machiavelli, writing in the sixteenth century, sums up the reality of organizational change (OC). However, defining the term is nearly as difficult as making it happen in reality!

For many people working in organizations, the question "What is OC and what does it mean?" is one that continually evades an answer. Individual views on the matter vary enormously, particularly once the discussion gets to a more detailed level.

This chapter looks at a number of perspectives. It discusses some of the unique characteristics of OC that make it such a challenging and fascinating area and, towards the end, defines terms closely related to OC.

Let's start with the big picture and some basics: the terms "organization" and "change". There are a number of models that define and describe an organization. These range from the "hard", mechanistic views through to the softer, more humanistic views, as detailed in the box below.

MODELS OF ORGANIZATIONS

» Machine/mechanistic - "just a set of cogs; turn the handle and out pops the product".
» Resource-based - an organization is a set of resources: finance, people, capability, etc.
» Systems - an organization is a system, or a number of interacting subsystems. There are a number of types: open, complex, complex adaptive, etc.
» Organism - an organization is a living thing, and subject to all the various drivers of evolution and survival.

> » Social – an organization is a collection of people. This includes,
>   therefore, the political-system model.
> » Human or psychological – an organization is a collection of
>   individuals.

These last two definitions focus on the human view of an organization. The others convey a more de-humanized view, and yet those are the models that people most commonly associate with the word "organization". When it comes to "change", all the dimensions represented here are important, as they can all influence change in organizations. However, the key points are that only people can initiate change, and that change can only happen *through* people. The converse is also true, i.e. that only people can inhibit change. People are therefore at the heart of organizations, and of change. This is important when considering the terms and definitions related to OC.

At the highest level there is a clear and common understanding as to what OC is.

The author defines OC as "the art, skill, process, or act of changing an organization in some planned, intentional way, with the purpose of improving its performance". This definition positions OC as a means of achieving an end or a desired result. A more simplistic definition is "the ability to turn ideas into reality, making things happen". The emphasis here is on execution – the most difficult aspect of any change and therefore the one most likely to be the cause of failure.

More conceptual definitions and interpretations are provided by academics. For example, Rosabeth Moss Kanter[1] defines it as "the crystallization of new action possibilities (new policies, new behaviors, new patterns, new methodologies, new products, or new market ideas) based on re-conceptualized patterns in the organization". Another more practical perspective comes from business practitioners such as Sir John Harvey-Jones[2], the leader of ICI in the 1980s. He states, "The role of leadership [in OC] is to really make the status quo more dangerous than launching into the unknown".

These are fine at a very general level. However, differences in the meaning and interpretation of OC arise at a lower, more detailed and practical level. The reasons for this arise from the unique nature of

OC in that it has no boundaries and cuts across *all* other functions and operations. It encompasses all other disciplines and areas of the business, such as human resources, leadership, business strategy, and project management.

As a result, OC is not a widely understood field, and is a particularly complex and ambiguous one.

One of the most simplistic definitions of OC suggests that its purpose is to address the following questions:

» why do we need to change?
» who is or should be involved?
» what needs to change, and what does it need to change to?
» how are we going to change?

Perceptions vary enormously over whether OC's primary role is to address all these questions, or just one or two. The commonest view today is that OC should simply address the last point – how are we going to change?

From an alternative perspective, we could see OC as a series of activities. Examples might be:

» finding a sponsor;
» conducting a change-readiness assessment;
» addressing the risks and issues arising from change;
» communicating to the main audiences; and
» defining a transition plan etc.

Given that people are central to organizations and change, another view sees OC as focusing on the psychology of change – on the areas of knowledge, motivation, commitment, and emotions.

In conclusion, it can be seen that OC is not a single entity that can be neatly defined. The term may refer to a single change or to a process of change(s), and encompasses a wealth of implications for investment, systems, structures, and people. Practically speaking, the fact that it eludes precise definition may not be that important. What matters is achieving the required change – more of that later!

It is helpful to have an understanding of related terms, and some are outlined below. (A word of caution – some terms are used interchangeably.)

» **Organization development (OD)** – a term that was popular in the 1980s but has recently fallen out of fashion. It describes the process of changing an organization to improve its effectiveness, through interventions aimed at improving its capability and competence. It is based on behavioral-science approaches, and was the precursor of the Change Management movement.
» **Organization design** – a term that refers to designing the structure of organizations and work at all levels – e.g. functions, divisions, teams, individual roles, and reporting relationships.
» **Organization behavior (OB)** – primarily a term used within academia referring to the ideas and concepts underpinning organizational performance. Examples include motivation, work design, etc.
» **Strategy** – a very common term but one that has a huge range of meanings. Generally it means "defining the direction, mission, goals, and purpose of an organization". Interpretation of this word can refer to both *what* to change and *how* to change. Usually, though, the intended meaning does not include the implementation of the strategy.
» **Strategic change** – a vague term generally used to mean the change implications of a strategy. By implication it refers to fairly wide-reaching change.
» **Change management** – a term typically used to describe how a change is achieved or executed.
» **Change agent** – a term applied to a broad set of roles, ranging from an individual who champions particular ideas, through to an executive who sponsors or leads initiatives and programs. The common thread in all change-agent roles is the fact that individuals make a personal commitment and take personal responsibility to see that actions are carried out.
» **Program management** – a term used to describe the high-level management of the program, focusing on the project management aspects such as resourcing and risks.

NOTES

1 Rosabeth Moss Kanter (1983) *The Change Masters*. Simon & Schuster, New York. Rosabeth Moss Kanter is discussed in more detail in Chapter 8 on "Key Concepts and Thinkers".
2 John Harvey-Jones (1989) *Making it Happen*. HarperCollins, London.

:

Evolution

- » Many factors have influenced the development of what we now know as OC.
- » The academic thinkers of the early twentieth century started the humanistic and social schools of thought.
- » Kurt Lewin was the true founder of OC at the end of the 1940s.
- » The field of OC is linked to many others, such as psychology, sociology, and strategy.
- » Relatively new schools of thought such as systems thinking have led the field of OC.
- » Until recently, academic interest has focused purely on the topic of strategy formulation.
- » The growth of technology within organizations has been a major catalyst for change in organizations.
- » The environment around organizations has been changing rapidly over the past 10 years.
- » Various management fads over the past decade have contributed both positively and negatively to the field of OC.
- » It is being increasingly recognized that the key factors in successful change are the softer, more intangible aspects of an organization, such as organizational culture.

"The factory of the future will have only two employees, a man and a dog. The man will be there to feed the dog. The dog will be there to keep the man from touching the equipment."

Warren Bennis

Warren Bennis was an early and key figure in the field of OC. Writing many books on the subject, he was the first to integrate both the leadership and the change perspectives for organizations. We'll talk more about him later.

This chapter provides an overview of the history and evolution of OC, charting its developments from the origins of man through to the present day. It is closely related to Chapter 8, which includes descriptions of the key thinkers and their ideas over the years. Chapter 6 details the state of the art and future trends.

The evolution of OC can be categorized into three distinct phases:

» **Phase 1**: the period up to the end of the 1960s;
» **Phase 2**: the 1970s and 1980s; and
» **Phase 3**: the 1990s.

The development of OC as a subject has been influenced by a broad range of factors, which include:

» social trends and patterns;
» academic writers and developing schools of thought;
» economic events and trends;
» the development and growth of commercial organizations;
» management fads, fashions and bandwagons;
» necessity; and
» developments in technology.

PHASE 1: THE PERIOD UP TO THE END OF THE 1960S

An interesting aspect of OC is that both components – organizations and change – have been with us for centuries. Since humans first walked on the earth, they have had to form teams and organize work to survive, develop, and prosper. Throughout history there has been a recurring pattern of the rise and fall of communities and civilizations, ranging from the Egyptians, Greeks, and Romans, to the Ottoman and later empires. Cycles and change are an inherent part of life.

The early part of the twentieth century saw a transition in management thinking. Writers before this time such as Taylor, Fayol, and Weber advocated a rather mechanistic and scientific approach to management and work. Their ideas gave way to ones from a new breed of thinkers, early pioneers such as Mary Parker Follet, Chester Barnard[1], and Elton Mayo[2]. They proposed a more humanistic and people-orientated approach to management. At the heart of these ideas was the concept of the organization as a social entity, attributing much of people's behavior to this "social" model, and thus recognizing the need to address the more human elements. Much of the work and many of the ideas produced in this period are still prevalent today, having influenced the thinking and lain the foundations for the field of OC.

Between the Second World War and the end of the 1960s, leading academics and thinkers developed these ideas further, pursuing research into fields closely related to OC – those of sociology, psychology, leadership, management, and work. These people included Douglas McGregor[3] (management styles), Abraham Maslow[4] (motivation), Rensis Likert[5] (leadership), Frederick Herzberg[6] (motivation), Edgar Schein[7] (psychology), Daniel Katz and Robert Kahn[8] (social psychology) and Igor Ansoff[9] (corporate strategy and change).

The real founder of the OC movement was Kurt Lewin[10], who in the late 1940s developed his three-step approach to change management: "Unfreeze, Change, and Re-freeze". This is discussed further in Chapter 8.

Further research on OC was not conducted until the early 1960s. In 1962 Warren Bennis, an early writer on change who later focused on the subject of leadership, wrote one of the first books specifically on OC, entitled *The Planning of Change*. He wrote another book in 1966 entitled *Changing Organizations*. Larry Greiner[11] wrote an article on what he referred to as the patterns of OC. Paul Lawrence[12] was one of the first people to investigate the subject of resistance to change, and came up with some key strategies in dealing with the issue. He then worked with Jay Lorsch[13] to write a number of important books and articles focusing on the relationship between organizations and the external environment, and how organizations might respond and adapt to changes in the latter.

In the 1960s organizations started to develop more formal organizational systems, strategies and structures. The idea of strategic planning started to become a more common and formalized process, with planning horizons of 10 years because of the relatively slow rates of change in the environment.

PHASE 2: THE 1970S AND 1980S

The 1970s started with the publication of a polemical book by Alvin Toffler[14] entitled *Future Shock*. This book forecast the huge changes in the social, economic, and technical areas of life. There was a tremendous growth in research and writing on OC and its related areas in this period, covering traditional areas such as organizations, strategy, and leadership as well as new disciplines such as Systems Thinking. There was too much output for us to cover all of it here, but we can outline some.

In the field of organizational strategy, several developments and thinkers influenced how organizations crafted strategy, and what the main components of any strategy were. In 1982 Peters and Waterman, two McKinsey consultants, wrote the classic book *In Search of Excellence*, which gave lessons from the best-run companies of the time, providing examples of how organizations were responding to the increasingly competitive and changing environment, and winning in it. These ranged from "a bias for action", through to "being close to the customer", and "sticking to the knitting". The idea of "incrementalism" as the ideal model for strategic planning became popular. This suggested that strategy and change were best achieved via incremental steps rather than big-bang transformations. At the time, given the relatively static external environment, this was accepted.

A few writers focused on the subject of change, the main interest being in the methodologies of change. Authors included Beckhard and Harris, who in 1977 wrote their classic book *Organizational Transitions*, articulating the idea of the "transition state" in change management.

Meanwhile, in the real world, organizations responded to pressures in the external environment in a number of ways. Some of the rapid shocks, such as the oil crises and economic fluctuations of the 1970s, highlighted the deficiencies of existing models. Organizations developed new techniques such as scenario planning methods, which were used successfully by Shell and other companies.

Management development started to grow, and at the same time, there was seen to be an increasing need to focus on the development of the organization as a whole, including areas such as structure, roles, functions, strategy development, and implementation. This led to the creation of Organizational Development (OD) teams in organizations. Chris Argyris[15] produced his seminal work on organizational learning and the barriers to learning and change. In parallel with this, the whole field of Systems Thinking, which had been around for many years (primarily in an engineering context), suddenly came to the fore in an organizational context. In the late 1980s Peter Checkland[16] devised Soft Systems Methodology (SSM), which introduced the concepts of cause, effect, and open systems. The associated methodologies were used widely for change programs, and spawned a wide range of derivatives.

W. Edwards Deming led the revolution in Quality, initially in Japan where they adopted many of his quality and statistical control techniques with great success. His ideas were then re-imported back into Western organizations. The challenge of the concept of quality was that it paid attention to widely different attributes of an organization's make-up or culture, both hard (focusing on measurement) and soft (focusing on behavior and attitude). The quality fad had a number of huge successes, and huge failures.

This led to a growing interest in the deeper, softer, more cultural aspects related to its success and implementation. Andrew Pettigrew[17], one-time CEO of ICI, suggested that "the shaping of organizational culture is the primary role of management". Edgar Schein also wrote about the importance and significance of organization culture in his classic book *Organizational Culture and Leadership*[7]. Other writers made the leap in logic to suggest that OC was very dependent upon the pervasive culture in organizations at the time.

Technology also started to have a growing impact on organizations. Developments in mainframe applications, such as databases, meant that their use was gaining wider acceptance. The development of the first PCs began to revolutionize the use and ownership of computing power. Software applications such as those for materials requirement planning started to impact organizations' purchasing and production operations. Compared with today's systems, these were small-scale. However, their planning and implementation started to raise major issues for organizations, and to establish the need for better planning of their introduction.

PHASE 3: THE 1990S

This period saw a continuation and escalation of a number of basic trends already apparent in the 1980s. In addition, other factors were starting to make an impact:

» the pressure on organizations to change was immense, whether because of globalization or of changing customer needs, increased competition or a change in regulation;

» the dramatically increased rates of change meant that organizations had to change faster than ever;

» the adoption of technology throughout the organization had never been greater, impacting all of its aspects and requiring it to change;

» the range and pressure of various stakeholder groups increased;

» organizations began to recognize that their real success came down to their "human capital" – the skills, qualities and talents of the individuals in the organization;

» harnessing and focusing employee talents and commitment was the real challenge of leadership;

» the demand for skills and talents exceeded supply, so that power shifted to the employee more than ever before;

» the various aspects of change were becoming increasingly connected, making decisions more complex; and

» there was an increasing adoption of various fads and bandwagons, promulgated by academics and consultancies alike.

All these trends had significant implications concerning the change agenda for the organizations and their people. They resulted in a considerable growth of the need for OC, and of its importance.

The fad that, initially at least, had most impact on organizations was that of Business Process Re-engineering (BPR), initiated by Champy and Hammer, two consultants working at the business consultancy CSC. The basic idea was to cut out many "antiquated" business processes, streamlining business operations and thereby doing away with many people. Since its heyday, this idea has proved to have had disastrous consequences for organizations. Interestingly, from an OC perspective, two of the contributing factors were deemed to be:

» lack of any significant people involvement or engagement in the change process (almost the opposite, in fact), resulting in people becoming fearful and cynical of any OC initiatives; and
» a focus on the short-term, financial cost-cutting benefits, rather than the longer-term growth potential of the organization.

Another driver was technology. This has been a huge factor over the last 10 years. Projects ranged from large-scale IT systems implementation through to the all-pervasive impact of the World Wide Web (WWW) and the Net. Within this field in the 1990s were a number of relevant trends, including ERP (Enterprise Resource Planning) systems, CRM (Customer Relationship Management) systems, and Supply Chain and Procurement systems. More recently the WWW and Web-enabled applications have enabled intranets and extranets to hook up all parties in the value chain. These projects have typically had a poor success record of creating business value when compared with the size of the investment. There are many reasons for this, but a common factor has been the challenges caused by the management of organizational and human issues.

A number of both established and new thinkers, writers, and academics made exciting and interesting contributions to the subject in this period. In almost complete opposition to the BPR fad, the concept of the learning organization came to the fore with Peter Senge's brilliant book *The Fifth Discipline*, followed up by *The Dance of Change*. Both these books built on the original concepts of the learning organization and soft-systems thinking. These themes have huge and powerful implications for OC.

The subject of organizational culture, which started to feature when quality was being emphasized in the 1980s, grew in interest. It could be looked at from the perspective of a company's vision, or through to its values and beliefs. Leading thinkers here include Collins and Porras, with their book *Built to Last*.

Table 3.1 charts the evolution of the subject of OC over the last 50 years.

Table 3.1   Time-line for OC.

Year	Event
1900s	Start of the Organizational Behavior movement
1930s	The Hawthorne experiments conducted by Mayo
	The Great Depression
	Publication of Chester Barnard's book *The Functions of the Executive*
1940s	Publication of Kurt Lewin's book *Frontiers in Group Dynamics*
1950s	Trend towards Management by Objectives
1960s	Project Management techniques – PERT and critical path analysis start to be widely used
	Douglas McGregor introduces Theory Y
1970s	Chris Argyris introduces Double-Loop learning
	OD becomes popular
	Human Resources replaces Personnel functions
	Publication of Alvin Toffler's book *Future Shock*
	Kotter's & Schlesinger's HBR article, ''Strategies for Change''
1980s	Publication of Peters' & Waterman's book *In Search of Excellence*
	Start of the Merger and Acquisition trend
	Start of Change Management
	Publication of Rosabeth Moss Kanter's book *The Change Masters*
	Publication of Tom Peters' book *Thriving on Chaos*
	Quality and TQM approaches start to gain popularity
1990s	Publication of Peter Senge's book *The Fifth Discipline*
	Hammer & Champy start the Business Process Re-engineering movement
	Introduction of Kaplan and Norton's Balanced Scorecard concept
	The Internet starts to make an impact
	Start of the trend to virtual organizations
	Start of the ERP system revolution
	Publication of Peter Senge's book *The Dance of Change*
	Publication of John Kotter's book *Leading Change*
	Corporate downsizing starts to become popular
2000	Knowledge Management becomes a reality
	The dotcom boom ends

NOTES

1 Chester Barnard (1938) *The Functions of the Executive*. Harvard University Press, Cambridge, MA.

2 Elton Mayo (1949) *The Social Problems of an Industrial Civilization*. Routledge, Boston, MA.

3 Douglas McGregor (1960) *The Human Side of Enterprise*. McGraw-Hill, New York.

4 Abraham Maslow (1970) *Motivation and Personality*. Harper & Row, New York.

5 Rensis Likert (1961) *New Patterns of Management*. McGraw-Hill, New York.

6 Frederick Herzberg, Bernard Mausner, & Barbara Bloch Snyderman (1959) *The Motivation to Work*. John Wiley & Sons, New York.
Frederick Herzberg (1966) *Work and the Nature of Man*. World Publishing Company, Cleveland. OH.
(1968) "One more time: How do you motivate employees?" *Harvard Business Review*, Jan – Feb, 53–62.

7 Edgar Schein (1965) *Organizational Psychology*. Prentice-Hall, Englewood Cliffs, NJ.
(1992) *Organizational Culture and Leadership*, 2nd edn. Jossey-Bass, San Francisco, CA.

8 Daniel Katz & Robert Khan (1963) *The Social Psychology of Organizations*. John Wiley & Sons, New York.

9 Igor Ansoff (1987) *Corporate Strategy*, revised edn. Penguin, London.
(ed) (1969) *Business Strategy*. Penguin, London.
(1976) *From Strategic Planning to Strategic Management*. John Wiley & Sons, New York.
(1979) *Strategic Management*. John Wiley & Sons, New York.
(1984) *Implanting Strategic Management*. Prentice-Hall, Englewood Cliffs, NJ.

10 Kurt Lewin (1947) "Frontiers in group dynamics: concept, method, and reality in social science, social equilibria, and social change." *Human Relations*, 1(1), 5–41.

11 Larry Greiner (1967) "Patterns of organizational change." *Harvard Business Review*, May – June, 119–130.

12 Paul Lawrence (1954) "How to deal with resistance to change." *Harvard Business Review*, May - June, 49-57.

13 Paul Lawrence & Jay Lorsch (1986) *Organization and Environment: Managing differentiation and integration*. HBSP, Boston, MA.
(1969) *Developing Organizations: Diagnosis and action*. Addison Wesley, New York.

14 Alvin Toffler (1970) *Future Shock*. Random House, New York.
(1980) *The Third Wave*. Morrow, New York.

15 Chris Argyris (1977) "Double-loop learning in organizations." *Harvard Business Review*, Sept - Oct, 115-124.

16 Peter Checkland (1980) *Systems Thinking, Systems Practice*. John Wiley & Sons, Chichester, UK.

17 Andrew Pettigrew (1985) *The Awakening Giant: continuity and change at ICI*. Blackwell, Oxford.

The E-Dimension

» Technology is becoming all-pervasive in organizations.
» It is precisely this pervasiveness that is the key issue for OC.
» Its impact on organizations is becoming increasingly significant.
» The implication is that the whole organization has to undergo change.
» The technology aspect is a small part of the overall change in an organization.
» The example of GE's "DYB" or "destroy-your-own-business.com" initiative is given as an example of best practice.
» This was so effective because it was led from the top, was totally integrated with business-as-usual, and had a very compelling case for action.

"And the trouble is, if you don't risk anything, you risk even more."

Erica Jong

These next two chapters focus on two key drivers in the external environment that are having a significant impact on organizations, on their strategies, and consequently on OC. In this chapter our focus is on the impact of technology, particularly the Internet and e-commerce; in the next we will focus on the impact of globalization.

We begin with a brief summary of the recent developments of the Internet and the "e" phenomenon: what they mean, together with an outline of the unique attributes that have led to their combined rise as a dominant revolutionary force in organizations. We discuss the major issues that the development of the Internet and e-business raise for organizations and OC. Finally, a case study examines how one organization – General Electric (GE) – responded to the Internet, through the creation of its "destroy-your-business.com" initiative.

The development and adoption of technology over the last decade has been breathtaking. Technology and its applications have been seen as a catalyst and enabler for improved business performance. They have offered greater functionality and increased automation, leading to increased productivity and performance levels. The influence of technology on organizations has been huge in a number of ways, some anticipated and some not. Its implementation has inevitably led to changes in areas such as business processes, roles, skills, and organizational structures. As a result, the assimilation of IT has been a real catalyst for OC and a driver for it.

The Internet, and in particular the WWW, has in a few years transformed our ability to manage information. The technology of the Net is relatively basic. What the Web offers is a unique set of characteristics and properties that make it very easy to process and communicate knowledge and information. These properties include:

» its cost, which is practically free;
» its ubiquitous, pervasive nature, accessible everywhere;
» its simple ease of use;
» its standardized and open nature as a platform;

» the speed with which a user can gain information; and
» the amount of information available.

As the Net explodes, increasingly the issues to be faced are those of structuring and filtering the knowledge it contains in order to obtain exactly the information required.

These fundamental characteristics have huge implications for organizations and for change. And the Web is only the beginning; current developments are focusing on the automation of the transactions that are the life-blood and cost of organizations.

The design and implementation of more sophisticated and complex e-business applications is of course not quite so simple. Within commercial organizations the transition to full Web-enabled e-commerce is taking place in a number of clear phases:

Phase 1 the creation of a Web site or Web presence – primarily for promotion;
Phase 2 the adoption of basic Web-based "front-end" sales applications;
Phase 3 the early adoption of e-business, integrated and automated IT systems; and
Phase 4 the total Web-enabling of a business, in both its customer-facing and its internal/back-office operations.

It is suggested that only 5% of all organizations are anywhere near Phase 4. Most are positioned somewhere in Phase 1 or 2, so the implications and changes are still in their infancy. What, then, are the longer-term implications for organizations? The original thinking was that the Internet required organizations to re-assess every aspect of their nature. This was revolution, changing everything – from business models, to strategies, to structures, processes, and operations, through culture, values, and purpose, to brand, sales, fulfillment channels and beyond. It was likened to throwing a pack of cards up in the air and watching where they landed.

However, more recent trends have shown that these prophecies were ill-founded. The Internet is possibly not quite as profound as people made it out to be. The traditional considerations of business are still key – money, revenues, customers, service, and profits. The traditional "bricks and mortar" companies are now beginning to embrace the Net, and to use it to facilitate more of the fundamentals of business, such as attracting, selling to, and retaining customers.

So, with our current view of the world, what are the most important implications for organizations when considering the implementation of e-business?

Organizations need to recognize that e-business has the potential to automate most, if not all, of a company's basic transactions, throughout the entire end-to-end process from promotion, through sale and fulfillment, to money collection. It has the potential to make information totally transparent, so that anyone can see whatever information they want to see. This has the knock-on effect of reducing internal organizational boundaries. Users or customers can conduct their own transactions, rather than having a representative of the organization do it for them – resulting in many benefits for the organization, including huge cost-savings, and making it easy for customers to manage the process. It opens up potential new sales channels, generating new revenue streams. From all of this, it is clear that the e-world has the potential to cut costs dramatically.

Don Tapscott, in his book *The Digital Economy*, defined five levels of change caused by the e-world and the Internet. These were:

1 the effective individual;
2 the high-performance team;
3 the integrated organization;
4 the extended enterprise – extranet, SCM, CRM; and
5 the inter-networked business – a networked value chain.

In some respects the implications of technology and the Internet on organizations and change are no different from those of any other form of OC.

The most significant OC issues that are unique to the Internet and the e-world are:

» the size and scale of the change, which is huge and really is "a revolution";
» the complexities associated with such a transition, the degree of interconnectivity in the change, and the knock-on effects;
» the fact that this is not something that can be done piecemeal – everything interconnects, everything has to change, and it all has to

happen at the same time, so the possibilities for incremental change are reduced;

» the impact on people within the organization – their jobs, roles, and skills, and the learning curve people will have to go through in order to appreciate the implications; and

» (leading on from these factors) more fundamental leadership and management questions such as "How do we do this? How do we manage this change?".

The solutions to these issues are:

» to place an increased emphasis on a more holistic and integrated approach;

» to ensure that any initiative or project is a fully integrated component of the rest of the organization's strategy;

» to think things through fully before embarking on grand schemes, which includes setting clear deliverables related to business goals for each project;

» to get commitment, ownership, and buy-in from all stakeholders and all parts of the organization;

» to communicate to everyone the rationale, business case, and reasons for the program and investment, and to continue that communication through the lifecycle of the project;

» to monitor progress; and

» to consider the potential risks and barriers to any project, assessing its feasibility and taking into account the resources available, the size of challenge, the set goals etc.

BEST-PRACTICE CASE STUDY – GE'S DESTROY-YOUR-BUSINESS.COM

This case study details the response of America's General Electric (GE) to the Internet revolution. It provides an example of best practice for OC, when considering the whole OC life cycle, revolving around initiating, managing, and sustaining OC.

This is a story of a large conglomerate's response to a trend whose impact is even now unclear. It provides many lessons for others to follow – clear executive leadership and sponsorship, the creation of a clear and compelling "burning platform", clear goals, and engaging, focusing, and aligning the whole organization behind the strategy.

Jack Welch needs no introduction, as he is seen by many as the best example of a corporate leader in recent times. GE is a huge organization, consisting of a diverse range of businesses, operating in both business-to-business (B2B) and business-to-customer (B2C) markets. Its divisions range from its airplane-engine business, to the broadcaster NBC, and to its finance arm, GE Capital.

Despite GE's performance and stature, it was slow to see and react to the significance of the Web and the Internet revolution. Although some of its divisions were involved in computer technologies, and some of its businesses had started to adopt some of the ideas and applications of the Net, the overall impact of the Net within GE was not recognized.

One of the reasons for this was the strategy that had led to its initial success: the decision to compete only in market segments where GE was either number one or number two.

It was not until Christmas 1998, when Jack Welch noticed his family buying presents over the Web for the first time, that he suddenly got the message, the light bulbs came on, and GE went into action. Early in 1999, Jack's blunt message to his divisions was "change your business model, or someone else will". The banner "DYB", or "destroy-your-business.com" was created and used to great effect in getting the message home to all parts of the GE business. Jack took personal ownership of this initiative. Inherent in the Internet revolution is a fundamental re-think of many basic tenets of an organization. For instance, what happens to branding when all things begin to become integrated and joined-up?

Full-time DYB teams were created in each of the business divisions to plan, oversee, and implement e-strategies.

Even with this limited background, there are many lessons that can be learned from this case study:

» the importance of sensing trends in the external environment, and of assessing their potential development and impact;
» the importance of real, active, top-level support and sponsorship;
» the recognition that action is absolutely key to the business;
» the recognition of a clear, compelling need to change;
» the importance of symbolic acts;

» the power of creating a unique brand for the change;
» clear communication;
» a top-down approach;
» an effective mix and balance of empowering staff, devolving decision-making, and clear top-down leadership;
» setting a clear direction;
» asking for action from each division head;
» setting clear goals and targets;
» allocating and aligning resources behind the initiative;
» implementing a range of incentives; and
» establishing champions at all levels in the organization to push for what they believe (see the first case study in Chapter 7).

The Global Dimension

» Globalization is an increasingly important issue for organizations.
» Its significance and implications are huge.
» Attributes of culture – especially national and organizational – are significant for OC.
» Sony is used as an example of best practice.
» Sony adopted a localized approach to change, and had a very participative element.

"The level of thinking that got us into this mess is not the level of thinking that will get us out."

Albert Einstein

This chapter considers the implications of globalization on organizations and change. It follows a format similar to that of the previous chapter, starting with an overview of the dimensions of globalization, and considering its key drivers. It then looks at the implications of globalization for organizations and change – how they are responding to these forces, and some of the issues they face. Finally we use Sony as an example of best practice.

Globalization is a well-used but poorly defined term. In a BBC broadcast in 1996, Peter Jay defined globalization as "the circumstances in which any entrepreneur, anywhere, can draw upon savings accumulated anywhere, and on the management skills and technologies located anywhere, to create a productive unit anywhere, employing local labor and selling its product anywhere to everyone".

There are many aspects and dimensions to globalization – its characteristics and dynamics are complex. These can be grouped into three areas:

» the company;
» the group(s) of people; and
» the approach to change.

Company-related elements include:

» its products or offers;
» its operations and locations;
» its strategy;
» its brand;
» its resources;
» its style, culture, systems, and structures;
» the degrees of freedom and autonomy it gives to people and operations;
» its styles of leadership and management; and
» how decisions are made.

The elements relating to people include:

» their culture – the history, values, beliefs, and norms of a group;

» their language and native styles; and
» their response and reaction to change.

Change-related elements include:

» the degree of involvement;
» representation;
» the emphasis given both to the "hard" elements of change (financials, targets, numbers) and to the "soft" ones (human);
» the degree of commitment; and
» the degree of choice, freedom and autonomy over the approach to be adopted, ranging from "one single way" through to multi-choice approaches – to accommodate all needs and styles.

Globalization impinges on the largest commercial multinationals and on a variety of agencies at national, regional, and global levels. It is seen both as an opportunity, and increasingly as a threat in some quarters. The complexity associated with globalization makes its trends and drivers difficult to understand and predict. They raise many difficult questions for organizations. An organization's response to these trends, and its ability to change, will determine its future success. The implications of globalization for organizations are far more company-specific than those of the Internet. The latter are generally the same for all organizations across the world.

Two main drivers influence globalization. One is finance and economics, related to the ever-increasing demand for returns and profits. Commercial organizations are looking to maximize revenues and minimize costs, through the development of offerings targeted at as large a market as possible. This means expanding into other geographies. At the same time they are trying to minimize competition and to achieve global scale and reach. This has been helped by the creation of the "global village" where there is now largely a single common language, and where geography is now largely irrelevant through excellent communications and transport. Distribution across the globe is fast, efficient, cheap, and reliable; and customers and markets are becoming more homogenous as time goes on.

The other main driver is the more human element, the growth of materialism and Western consumerism, which seeks to address the need for attention and relationships through the acquisition of material goods and icons.

There are some major barriers to globalization, the most significant of which relate to characteristics of particular societies such as language, culture, standards, norms, or beliefs. There are also barriers associated with nation states and with the associations and trading blocs they form, such as ASEAN, NAFTA, and the EU, together with the global organizations or agencies such as the World Trade Organization, the World Bank, and the IMF. In this interconnected world, organizations are an integral part of the system, partly being influences within it, and partly reacting to it.

The globalization trend creates many challenges and problems for organizations and the people within them. These issues revolve around judgements and decisions on matters of OC – what to change, what to change to, how to change, who to change, and (particularly with globalization) where to change. These are not simple issues, as the nature of the considerations and options are complex and interdependent. The issues will largely depend on the nature and characteristics of the particular organization and on its competitive environment. For example, a global multinational will face issues very different from those facing a small organization currently operating only in its home market but wishing to expand its reach and to enter overseas markets with its existing products. Whatever the organization, decisions have to be made on a broad range of matters related to the organization's composition.

Organizations' responses to the issue of globalization vary enormously, and are again very company-specific. A small organization wanting to expand into new markets may open a local sales office in a new potential market as part of a globalization strategy. On the other hand, a large multinational may decide to centralize or consolidate certain operations into a single location. Some may want to switch from a national brand and attempt to create a single global brand, while others may attempt to create global business units with regional operations. Some may decide to roll out standardized systems, processes, and policies across their global operations. All will involve a considerable amount of OC.

GLOBALIZATION AS A DRIVER FOR OC

Globalization can be viewed as just another driver for OC. In many respects the aspects of OC relating to globalization are the same as for any other OC:

» why change?
» who to change;
» what to change, and to what; and
» how to change.

However, globalization raises some unique and particularly difficult issues for OC. One of the most significant is the greatly increased number and variety of stakeholders who are either impacted or involved.

Related to this is the matter of having to deal with a much wider range of differences and diversity – in terms of people's language, their culture and styles, and their beliefs and values. It is important to see this as something of value, rather than taking the easier reaction of viewing it as a problem and an issue. Achieving a high and wide degree of involvement and participation is crucial in these situations.

The increase in the number and diversity of stakeholders influences the third main difficulty, the degree of complexity then involved in any change. This is not helped by the issue of "managing the matrix" – that is, managing the views of the three main groups:

» geographical or national;
» product or business; and
» functional – sales, marketing, production etc.

An important element in OC is balancing the needs of local customers with those aggregated from global markets. It is important not to alienate particular groups for whatever reason, but rather to gain support, commitment, and buy-in across the organization. A key factor here is the composition of project and change teams. There is a need to ensure a flexibility of approach and the local adoption of any changes, requiring a means of getting input into decisions in order to ensure that local differences are understood and dealt with.

Two-way communication and information flows – up and down, and to and from the center – can be a real issue. Factors such as language, understanding, and the time or priority given to these types of events are often forgotten or given low priority.

This raises the question of management and leadership styles: who is in charge, what style is adopted, how the style manifests itself and is seen by others with different backgrounds, nationalities and so on. In these situations a broad range of leadership and management styles is appropriate.

Lastly, there are the questions of decision making within these situations, and the time, cost, and energy involved in bringing people together and in making things happen across the globe.

At the heart of any OC in response to globalization issues should be the focus on representation and people issues. As much as possible, people should be engaged throughout the whole process, understanding the issues and their implications, defining the possible options and alternatives available, making decisions and implementing them. All stakeholders should be engaged, representing as wide a range of people and views as possible. An integral part of this should be a real focus on communications within, across, and to the whole organization. Great care should be taken not just to see the global view, but also to see and understand the views at as local a level as possible.

An obvious approach is to forgo a common, global solution, and instead allow local groups to define their own local solutions and implementation. This requires giving a high degree of subsidiarity and autonomy to local operations. However, this is vital if a strategy is to be implemented successfully.

BEST-PRACTICE GLOBAL-CHANGE CASE STUDY – SONY "LOCAL GLOBALIZATION"

Sony is a classic example of an organization that has become truly global. Since its creation in Japan over 55 years ago in the aftermath of World War Two, its success, in terms of its growth, products, brand, diversity, and market leadership, is indisputable.

The Japanese culture is of course partly influential in Sony's success, but another key reason has been the company's ability to accommodate, adopt, and learn from the best of other cultures and ways of doing things – almost to "go native" at every possible opportunity. It was the co-founder of Sony, Akio Morita, who coined the phrase "local globalization" that was to become synonymous with Sony's approach, and who led the way for other organizations to follow. Sony was one of the early pioneers in the electronics field, purchasing rights to the transistor soon after it was invented. It started to make transistor radios, and then moved on to producing TVs. Once it had penetrated its home market in Japan it decided to expand into foreign markets, starting in the US, but quickly moving to the rest of the world.

Some of the reasons for Sony's success can be attributed to the culture and style of its management. Ambiguity and uncertainty are accepted as norms. Emphasis is placed on having a long-term strategy or direction, defined within a broad framework, which is adjusted incrementally. That is not to say that Sony cannot turn and has not turned quickly in response to new information. Within the strategy there is a balanced view of performance, where short-term financial results are only one of the indicators influencing strategic decisions. There are very high levels of creativity and innovation. One of the ways in which this is achieved is through the process of cross-fertilization, such as by adopting and sharing best-practice ideas from within the business, or by moving managers around different business groups to gain and widen their experience.

Also inherent in the way of doing business in Sony is a constant questioning and challenging of the norms, assumptions, and perspectives. This ensures that the organization is in touch with what is happening. Lastly, there is a very high degree of involvement and participation in the discussion of issues and solutions.

However, what Sony did so well and so successfully in those early days of expansion overseas was to adopt a number of broadly based policies that ensured that local perspectives were obtained at all possible levels.

» There was no single, fixed model of organizational structure. They adopted a more contingency-based approach. For example, the different business and manufacturing groups were all organized differently, according to the needs and characteristics of the particular business and Sony's operations.

» They accepted the value of diversity and the adoption of differing approaches, drawing on local knowledge and expertise.
» Decision-making was highly devolved, with a high degree of autonomy.
» Local staff and management ran the operations.
» A highly matrixed structure led to a quite informal style of corporate governance. Again, the organizational structure was highly devolved and unique to particular business groups.
» Sony's style was very participative – they were one of the first Japanese organizations to have non-nationals on their Boards.
» Documentation, brochures etc. were created in the local languages of key markets.
» They were willing to adapt to particular local circumstances and issues.

It is interesting to compare this with the typical American approach to problem solving, decision making, and execution. Americans generally have little participation, reach quick decisions, but then take a long time over implementation. Contrast this with the Japanese style, which has lots of participation, is slow to make a decision, but is then fast to execute it. The Japanese theme is continued in Chapter 7, when the Japanese state is used as a case study. There are some excellent books on Japanese management and on Sony in particular. Examples are:

» Akio Morita (1988) *Made in Japan*. Harper Collins, London.
» Richard Pascale (1981) *The Art of Japanese Management*. Simon & Schuster, New York.
» William Ouchi (1981) *Theory Z*. Addison-Wesley, Reading, MA.

The State of the Art

OC currently faces a number of issues:

» the disconnection between strategy and OC;
» widely varying levels of understanding, interpretation, and recognition of its value;
» the myriad of barriers to change;
» how to assess the amount of change; and
» the constancy and speed of change.

There are a number of new ideas, themes, and trends within OC:

» broad-based participation;
» a more integrated and holistic approach to change;
» balancing the coercive and participative approaches to change;
» an acknowledgement that there are different types of change – for instance, superficial and deep;
» measurement;
» change capability; and
» systems thinking.

In England in the 1950s, the Royal Artillery was giving a demonstration to some visiting Europeans. The visitors were most impressed with the speed and precision of the artillery crew, but one visitor asked about the duty of the man who stood at attention throughout the demonstration.

"He's number six," an officer explained.

"But why is he there?" the visitor enquired.

"That's his job. Number six stands at attention throughout."

"But why not just have five?"

No one knew, and only after a thorough search of the old manuals did they finally discover his duty: he was the one who held the horses.

Chapter 2 introduced the subject of organizational change (OC) and set out some key terms and definitions. Chapter 3 then gave a historical perspective on the evolution of the subject. This chapter brings that coverage up to date. It discusses some of the biggest OC issues faced by organizations and their teams. It then details the latest and best ideas that have emerged in the subject to date. Finally it considers future trends in the field.

ISSUES IN OC TODAY

The poor connection between strategy formulation and implementation

Corporate strategy has tended to be solely concerned with defining the future direction and, at best, the goals of an organization, with competition and customer trends as primary inputs, somewhat in isolation from anything else. Invariably it is constructed by a small group of top executives. This select group, having considered the data and generated a number of options, then proudly announce their strategic decisions to the rest of the organization. This is accompanied by a project plan given to middle management to implement.

This approach is one of the reasons for corporate strategy's failure over recent years, and the subsequent difficulties experienced in implementation. It has two major failings, related to change management:

» There is no input from elsewhere in the organization, nor a check on its capacity or capability, and therefore there is a poor understanding of what is possible, feasible, and realistic.

» The strategy formulation process has not been concerned with the dirty work of how to implement or realize the strategy. Strategy formulation and implementation have been seen as a linear process with two distinct activities, separated by time, people, and roles.

A clear and common understanding of what OC is

Chapter 2 highlighted the issue of the poor understanding of what OC is. There is no real common understanding of it, nor an accepted definition. This situation is exacerbated by OC's rather gray, vague nature. Even today there are very few real OC functions in organizations, although OC consultants work for some of the larger and more specialist change-consultancies.

The low importance attached to the role and value of OC

OC suffers from a low perception of its importance and added value. It is fair to say that there are many challenges involved in articulating, measuring, and defining the contribution, degree of success, and value of OC. A poor approach to measurement inevitably comes from a poor understanding of what OC is. It is then self-limiting and results invariably in a high-level planning decision that it is one cost that is not needed – that the cost of doing it outweighs the cost of not doing it. This is the complete opposite of the correct decision. This factor is closely related to the next one.

Roles and responsibilities within OC

The core activities within the process of OC are relatively well-established. However, the roles and responsibilities within an OC program and the boundaries between them are not so clear or so well-defined. These roles include both formal ones such as that of the program manager, and informal ones such as those of the change champions. There are a number of real and practical reasons for this, including the overlaps between the "steady-state" business structures and the project-team structures. It is evident that at times confusion and conflict exist between the members of the program team, along with disputes over who is responsible for what – particularly if the program starts hitting problems and delays.

One school of thought suggests that the sponsor with overall responsibility should take a particular interest in the OC aspects. Others suggest that OC is something that project managers should handle as part of their job, or that it is the remit of the HR group. These approaches are fine as long as the appropriate resources, skills, and priorities are given.

People and their roles or responsibilities are an absolutely fundamental issue in ensuring that change is successful. One-to-one coaching is common for someone taking on a change role, because of the differences from any business-as-usual role.

Questions about who does what, who is responsible for what, or where roles overlap inevitably bring a power perspective into play.

Addressing the barriers to change

There are always many barriers to any change. They comprise a number of elements. The first is the conflict and tensions between "business as usual" and "building for tomorrow and change". All organizations face this challenge of trying to survive today at the same time as changing to meet tomorrow's needs and demands. Pressure invariably focuses on achieving today's results, with building for tomorrow coming in second. Achieving a balance between the two is never easy.

The second barrier revolves around changing the status quo. This huge consideration is usually vastly underestimated. All sorts of forces and mechanisms are at work to try to maintain the status quo. Machiavelli's quote at the head of Chapter 1 is illustrative of this.

A further barrier concerns resistance to change – the reasons and causes for people's resistance are interesting and varied, such as "I'll lose my job", "I'll be worse off", "I don't agree with the solution", or "I don't know what to do now". Most of the resistance to change can be addressed, and with suitable creativity and flexibility a win–win situation can usually be found.

Creating a feasible change program and providing sufficient resources

The rates of success of change programs are dismally low. Research suggests that approximately 70% of change programs fail, and a further 20% do not meet the anticipated expectations of their sponsors.

The most important issue is one of executing the change:

» realizing the planned benefits;
» seeing things through;
» estimating the size of change, and how much energy and resources it will take;
» establishing and persisting with a commitment;
» balancing the wide and diverse range of stakeholder needs and demands;
» adopting a style – consulting or telling;
» getting faster;
» being realistic about abilities and the feasibility of change initiatives;
» underestimating time, resources, and difficulty;
» coordinating and integrating all the change activities, producing a unified whole; and
» running parallel activities.

The paradox of leadership – caught between a rock and a hard place

Senior executives and leaders are only human – the "superhuman" myth of leaders has been proven to be false. Each is but one person, who in a large organization is charged with a near impossible challenge. Leaders strive to be everything to everyone and yet they know they cannot be. They are expected to delegate, get involved, sponsor, empower, and provide a vision and strong leadership, yet support bottom-up change. Theirs is a hard job.

Managing the people factor

Change only really takes place at the personal level. The extent to which an individual buys into, commits to, and embraces a change depends on a large range of factors. Principal amongst them is the degree of the individual's involvement in the decision, solution, or approach to the change. Here we are considering the very human factors and qualities associated with the change. The biggest criticism and cause of resistance is the fact that people are not involved, represented, or consulted enough.

» Everyone has a personal agenda.
» In change there are always winners and losers, and quite rightly the losers will fight.
» People all have different views and opinions, which constantly influence the agenda and outcomes.
» People do not stay in the same jobs. They move on, while new people come in with different perspectives, and so new decisions are made.

Constant change – change on top of change

One of the biggest issues is that once a strategy and its associated change have been decided, it is overtaken by a further change to the situation or circumstances, or by events. This results in another change in the goals, focus, direction, or need. Possibly the change itself becomes redundant, or has a lower priority than it once had. Priorities shift and change - this impacts initiatives and resource allocation.

Speed of change

Given the increasing rate of change, a growing issue concerns the speed of change, particularly with regard to implementation. Speed - achieving change more quickly, with more immediacy and a faster return on investment - is becoming a hot topic.

Sustaining and embedding the change

Making the change stick is another real issue, particularly in projects focused on changing deep-rooted culture or style issues. The big launch is made, energy and resources are ploughed into the project, and then energy, attention, and focus drifts onto newer projects. Thus, just at the critical time, the rubber-band effect pulls the goals back into the bad old ways.

Coping with the increased scale and complexity of large projects

The increased complexity of a changing situation can be overwhelming – with things on a larger scale, more stakeholders, greater uncertainty, a broader set of factors/criteria/dimensions to manage, and paradoxes and dichotomies to cope with.

NEW IDEAS, THINKING, CONCEPTS, AND RESEARCH

Change is absolutely vital for the success of all organizations now. It is *the* agenda item of boardrooms today. Yet, to date, the success of change programs has been relatively low – as we mentioned in Chapter 1, evidence suggests only a 30% success rate. It is not surprising, then, that interest in and research into the success factors and causes of failure of change programs has never been greater. The main causes of failure have been described in the previous section.

What is interesting is that, for such a relatively old field as this, many of the results and conclusions from the new research fail to surprise or to give new insights into the field. The old chestnuts prevail. There are exceptions, of course. Chaos theory and complexity theory are supplying new insights into this fascinating field. This section details some of the new ideas and trends that are evolving in the area of OC as we move into the twenty-first century. Most are not rocket science, and many are not controversial. They are common sense, but not common practice.

The first aspect concerns the broad environment in which these planned changes are taking place. It is clear that we are entering a totally new area, with fundamentally new rules and new paradigms. This impacts both the formulation of strategy and its implementation.

Consider first the strategy formulation aspect. As the rate of change speeds up, it becomes more and more difficult to predict and forecast the future, which becomes less clear, more uncertain. This is brilliantly demonstrated by a curve Eddie Obeng[1] uses in which he defines "The New World". In the Old World, the pace of change was relatively slow, so planners could accurately predict the trends and patterns over the next few years, and the organization had time to make the minor re-adjustments that were needed. However, as the rate of change in the external environment speeds up, the organization's ability to change cannot keep up. This crossover point is occurring now, as illustrated in Fig. 6.1. The implications of this for an organization's strategy and approach to change are huge.

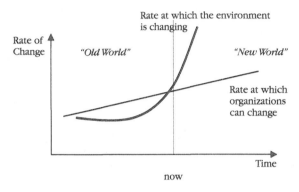

Fig. 6.1 The transition from the Old World to the New.

» Organizations now cannot "know" or predict the future.
» Even if they could, they would be unable to change quickly enough to keep up with the pace of change.

The knee-jerk response – throwing even greater amounts of resource into analysis and planning – will fail. We just don't know what the future holds, because no one can predict it. So what do we do? We make it up as we go along: we try, experiment, see what works, develop it, and if it doesn't work – we ditch it.

Rosabeth Moss Kanter,[2] in her new book *eVolve!*, promotes the use of improvisation as a strategic response. Long gone are the "strategic planners."

So, what is the current thinking on OC following on from the ideas above?

Broad-based participation and collaboration in formulating strategies and their implementation

There are a number of elements to this idea:

» getting more people and a broader mix of levels to be engaged and contributing to the strategic formulation process;
» getting more people engaged in the change process as a whole;
» getting ideas from a range of people; and
» pursuing a bottom-up approach to change.

"The peasants are revolting!" as the saying goes, and "You are either part of the problem, or part of the solution". Many executives harbor huge fears and concerns over getting more people involved in some of the key issues of the organization. Consider the views expressed about some of the EU representation legislation: they fear the worst – lazy employees, whose primary motive is to sabotage any difficult decisions or unpalatable options, ensuring that vested interests remain. Other concerns are that "It will create massive delays and take forever", or "They won't come up with the right answers". These are symptomatic of a range of beliefs, attitudes, and cultures that reflect a typical top team's view of strategy and change.

Jeannie Daniel Duck[3] in her latest book, *The Change Monster*, addresses the more human aspects associated with change. She talks about the degree of discretionary effort that managers and employees have to contribute to a change effort. She proposes asking the tough questions, such as "Why should I invest my time and energy in this change?". Historically, most change models, books, and approaches within organizations have adopted a very rational approach. Emotional aspects have not played a large or significant part to date. It is almost as if today the emotional aspects and factors are ignored – hidden under the surface. And yet, when dealing with people matters, the issues raised are primarily emotional. This is another theme from Duck's book – that emotions should play a greater role in the change. Emotional Intelligence (EQ) has become a popular concept since the publication of a book of the same name written by Daniel Goleman[4].

Two researchers, Michael Beer and Nitin Nohria[5], in their book *Breaking the Code of Change*, articulate two opposing theories on the approach or style of change, labeled Theory E and Theory O.

Theory E states that change should be achieved by focusing on hard numbers – letting financials drive the program. The opposite view, Theory O, states that change should be driven by and for employees, advocating maximum participation with members of staff.

Theory O is similar to the Learning Organization concept championed by Peter Senge[6], amongst others. He advocated in his book *The Fifth Discipline* that there were five learning disciplines:

» personal mastery;
» shared vision (aspiration);
» mental models;
» team learning; and
» systems thinking (covered later in the chapter).

Senge suggests that the key to change is learning, and that change starts with the individual. "Things" change only if the people change. People only change if they see the world differently, which means some form of personal development. The bottom line is that you cannot force people to change; they have to want to change. The challenge for organizations is to take their people through some form of program that enables them to understand what is happening, helps them to come to their own conclusions about the implications and options, and then supports them in the process of changing. This can take place at all levels – those of the individual, team, and organization – hence the term "Learning Organization".

A couple of other elements relate to the theme of greater broad-based participation. The first is the value and importance of bottom-up change. There is enormous value in getting everyone involved and engaged in the debate about future directions and change. Many writers have called for this, ranging from Duck who suggested an action of "stimulating conversation", through to Beer, Einstat & Spector who suggested "mobilizing energy for change through joint diagnosis of business problems".

The other main element relates to a growing social trend, that of the increasing importance and power of individuals. The implications for change are profound. In every area of change, there is an increasing awareness of the need to treat people as individuals – understanding, respecting, and working within the sphere of the individual. This requires a considerably greater degree of planning, tolerance, and flexibility. We need to get smarter at change – at understanding its complexities and subtleties, and adopting more sophisticated approaches to it.

This leads neatly on to the next trend within OC.

The call for more integrative and holistic approaches

There are a number of elements to this:

» aiming for greater integration and alignment across the organization – in terms of programs, moving away from the piecemeal approaches to strategy and change that have gone before;

» taking a more holistic approach when tackling any activity or dealing with information, including blurring the boundaries of roles and teams; and

» adopting more integrative approaches and models.

As a concept, the "integrative approach" is very compelling. It makes complete sense, and yet produces some difficult choices for those in charge of change.

There are very strong positive benefits for an organization adopting a broader approach and taking into account more of the factors and issues in impacting and influencing change. The only real downside is the amount of discussion and debate that is required to consolidate differing views, perspectives, and issues. This takes considerable time, energy, and resources. However, this approach is similar to that typically taken by the Japanese, who spend a considerable amount of time discussing, soliciting different views, and gaining consensus. The real advantage of this approach is that, having achieved a consensus and gotten everyone on board, the time to implement it is reduced significantly because there is much less resistance and many fewer surprises once implementation starts.

One approach that presents a number of options for any change is that of the "Change Kaleidoscope" (Fig. 6.2) created by Julia Balogun and Veronica Hope-Hailey[7], both from the Cranfield School of Management in the UK. Their model, introduced in their book *Exploring Strategic Change*, assumes that the "what" is predefined, and in defining the "how" it addresses the two perspectives of:

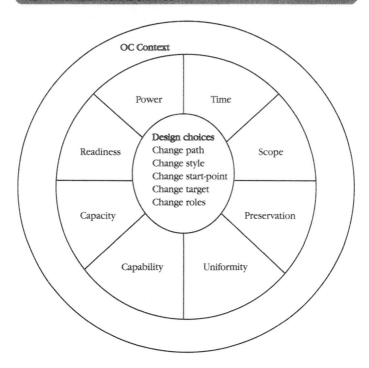

Fig. 6.2 The Change Kaleidoscope.

» the change context; and
» the change choices.

The change contexts are:

» scope;
» time;
» power;
» readiness;
» capacity;
» capability;

» uniformity; and
» preservation.

The Design Choices are:

» change path;
» change style;
» change start point;
» change target;
» change roles; and
» change levers.

A vital component of these process frameworks is the inherent set of management styles within them. This is an important issue.

Balancing the two extremes of leadership style – coercive and empowered approaches

Leaders are generally "damned if they do, and damned if they don't". It's a tough life leading an organization in these times, where the label "CEO" probably more accurately refers to "Change Executive Officer".

Much of the change literature, including this book, talks about maximizing employee and stakeholder involvement and participation. While this is true, there are important caveats. The armed forces operate primarily by means of command and control, where it is not the done thing to discuss or argue with the sergeant. Just so, in organizations in certain circumstances or times – invariably in urgent or crisis situations – leaders have to lead, and people simply have to do as they are told and follow orders. The fundamental question is: when is each of these styles appropriate?

In these times of increasing change, both styles are appropriate – but in different contexts, and for different reasons and purposes. People need to be told the nature of the givens, the constraints, and the overall goals. They then should be given the freedom, responsibility, and authority to act on them. Dunphy and Stace,[8] two Australian researchers, came up with an interesting model (Fig. 6.3) to help with this dilemma.

Related to change competence is the next new frontier – organizational culture.

	Incremental Change Strategies	Transformative Change Strategies
Collaborative Modes	Participative Evolution	Charismatic Transformation
Coercive Modes	Forced Evolution	Dictatorial Transformation

Fig. 6.3 A typology of change strategies, due to Dunphy & Stace.

Types of change: first- and second-order (cultural) changes

The type of change is a key issue in any OC. Interest has been growing in this area recently, primarily because of the need to understand the continued failure of most changes, which is now being linked to the type of changes that organizations are implementing. Also, as OC is now becoming so pervasive, it is slowly being recognized that no single approach will fit all the types of change.

The most interesting aspect is the recent differentiation between what is being labeled or characterized as superficial change and what as deep change. The former relates to organizational changes such as restructuring or the implementation of a standard system. The latter refers to changes that require a fundamental shift in attitude or behavior from a large percentage of the organization's employees. The latter type of program is far more difficult to achieve and sustain, precisely because it involves influencing and changing the deep-rooted attitudes, beliefs, and behavior of individuals.

A related development is that the fundamental barriers to major OC, and also its key enablers, are increasingly recognized to be the deep, cultural aspects. In analyzing why OC is so difficult, suffers from so many issues, and is so difficult to sustain, the concept of organizational culture surfaces as a root cause.

Many writers discuss culture and point out its profound importance and impact on organizations. While organizational culture is defined in many ways, Johnson and Scholes[9] provide a popular definition: the "cultural web", which comprises stories, symbols, rituals and routines, control systems, power structures, and the organizational structures associated with a particular organization.

In order to get effective, sustained, and long-term change, it appears that it is these cultural aspects of an organization that really have to be addressed.

From an academic point of view, Levy has defined two categories of change: first-order and second-order. Levy[10] defined first-order change as that which makes incremental adjustments but does not change the system's core. Second-order change involves altering the system's fundamental governing rules. Other labels that have been used for these two types include "evolution" and "revolution".

Jay Lorsch,[11] an early thought-leader in the cultural implications of change, wrote a brilliant article entitled "Managing Culture: the invisible barrier to strategic change" for the *Californian Management Review* in 1986. Edgar Schein[12] has written a number of books and articles on the subject of cultural change, one example being the article "Coming to a new awareness of organizational culture", published in the *Sloan Management Review* in 1984.

Measurement

A major issue for OC has been the inability to quantify change, particularly during the process of change itself – in other words, assessing its progress – apart from the status of the latest project plan. Usually there are very clear goals for any program, which can be assessed at its end.

A variety of trends have led to this renewed interest in measuring change. One source was Kaplan's Balanced Scorecard[13], with its ideas of lead and lag indicators. Interestingly, one of the four dimensions within the Balanced Scorecard was Learning and Innovation (the others being Customer and Market, Financial, and Internal Process). This links in with the other factors mentioned earlier – a focus on learning and a broader, more holistic and integrated approach to change. Another source comes from technology, where measurement tools and systems can be applied remotely, simply, and quickly via electronic forms of communication and tools. Such measurements can also be made confidentially, thus ensuring that real attitudes, thoughts, and feelings are captured, rather than "what the boss wants to hear".

There are now ways of quantifying and measuring the softer, more human aspects of a change and its progress. Useful metrics deal with knowledge of, commitment to, and support for a particular program.

Developing a change capability within an organization as a key competency

Hamel and Prahalad,[14] in their book *Competing for the Future*, first brought the idea of core organizational competencies to the attention of the business community. However, it is interesting that nothing was mentioned about a core organizational competency to do with leading and managing OC, possibly because it is something common to all organizations. The ability or competence to manage OC is becoming increasingly important in organizations. This is a theme that Peter Senge, author of *The Fifth Discipline* and *The Dance of Change*[15], believes is critical to an organization's future success, at both a personal and an organizational level.

Systems thinking, and chaos and complexity theories

Systems thinking provides a lot of the context and background for the newer sciences of chaos and complexity theories. These fields originated in the sciences closely related to nature. It seems that nature's own patterns are based on chaos and complex principles. Many business writers have started to apply these ideas to the fields of organizations and change. The first was probably Tom Peters[16] in his 1988 book *Thriving on Chaos*. More recent writers include Daryl Conner[17] with *Leading at the Edge of Chaos*, Richard Pascale[18] with *Surfing the Edge of Chaos*, Ralph Stacey[19] with *Complex Response Processes in Organizations*, and Brown and Eisenhardt[20] with *Competing on the Edge: Strategy as Structured Chaos*.

Some of these books start from a scientific viewpoint and relate this to management, while others have the field of management as their origin, and work the other way. The result is a mix of ideas, including some very useful practical ideas and tools as well as vague and rather conceptual ideas that loosely relate to change. Some improvisational techniques derive from a study into complex systems. This area is still in its infancy, but we can expect some important ideas and techniques to come out of this exciting and rapidly growing field.

NOTES

1 Eddie Obeng (1997) *New Rules for the New World*. Capstone, Oxford.

2 Rosabeth Moss Kanter (2001) *eVolve!*. HBSP, Boston, MA.

3 Jeannie Daniel Duck (2001) *The Change Monster*. Crown Business, New York.

4 Daniel Goleman (1995) *Emotional Intelligence*. Bantam, New York.

5 Michael Beer & Nitin Nohria (eds) (2000) *Breaking the Code of Change*. HBSP, Boston, MA.

6 Peter Senge (1990) *The Fifth Discipline*. Currency Doubleday, New York.

7 Julia Balogun & Veronica Hope-Hailey (1999) *Exploring Strategic Change*. FT/Prentice Hall, London.

8 Dexter Dunphy & Doug Stace (1988) "Transformational and coercive strategies for planned organization change: beyond the OD model." *Organization Studies*, Vol 9 No 3, 339-355.

9 Gerry Johnson & Kevan Scholes (1999) *Exploring Corporate Strategy*, 5th edn. Prentice Hall, Hemel Hempstead.

10 Amir Levy (1986) "Second-order planned change: definition and conceptualization." *Organisational Dynamics*, Vol 15 No 1 (Summer), 5-20.

11 Jay Lorsch (1986) "Managing culture: the invisible barrier to strategic change." *California Management Review*, Vol 28 No 2, Winter, 95-109.

12 Edgar Schein (1984) "Coming to a new awareness of organizational culture." *Sloan Management Review* Vol 25 No 2, 3-16.

13 Robert Kaplan & David Norton (1996) *The Balanced Scorecard: translating strategy into action*. HBSP, Boston, MA.

14 Gary Hamel & C.K. Prahalad (1994) *Competing for the Future*. HBSP, Boston, MA.

15 Peter Senge *et al.* (1999) *The Dance of Change*. Doubleday, New York.
16 Tom Peters (1987) *Thriving on Chaos*. Harper & Row, New York.
17 Daryl Conner (1988) *Leading at the Edge of Chaos*. John Wiley & Sons, New York.
18 Richard Pascale *et al.* (2001) *Surfing the Edge of Chaos*. Texere Publishing, London.
19 Ralph Stacey (2001) *Complex Responsive Processes in Organizations*. Routledge, London.
20 Shona Brown & Kathleen Eisenhardt (1998). *Competing on the Edge: strategy as structured chaos*. HBSP, Boston, MA.

In Practice

Three case studies outline some very important learning points from organizations' experiences. The three concern Jim, an individual change agent; the Daimler-Chrysler merger; and Japan's attempts to break out of its stagnation. Key learning points from these include the importance of:

» reinforcing structures;
» initiative;
» understanding where other people are coming from; and
» understanding and thinking through the amount of change involved.

"No plan survives contact with the enemy."

Field Marshal Helmuth von Moltke

This chapter provides some examples of organizational change (OC) in practice. They have been chosen to provide a range of different scenarios, contexts, styles, and issues that are commonly seen in OC. The three examples increase in scale and complexity, from an individual in an organization through to a whole nation state. They are:

1 an example of a change agent's attempt to initiate OC in the US;
2 an example of a global merger – DaimlerChrysler; and
3 an example of a broader scenario – that of Japan as a whole since the bubble burst over 10 years ago.

This chapter should be read in conjunction with Chapter 6, which focuses on the state of the art, together with Chapter 8, which describes key concepts, and Chapter 10, which defines a 10-step plan for making OC work.

CASE STUDY 1: JIM, THE AGENT OF CHANGE

This case study tries to bring out experiences and learning at a personal level, demonstrating how an individual at relatively junior levels in an organization can make a significant impact and contribution to re-orientating an organization's strategy and results.

Pluto Inc was a medium-sized US software organization selling ERP (Enterprise Resources Planning) and supply-chain systems to medium-sized businesses. It employed 2000 people and had two main products. It was organized in the traditional manner, with a board whose reporting functions included R&D, Sales, and Marketing. It had departments for Product Management, Support and all the various back-office functions. Its go-to-market channels were via a direct sales force focusing on the larger corporates, and a small number of agents focusing on medium-sized corporates. The company was 10 years old, and had been formed by two software engineers from IBM. Sales and customers had been growing at a year-on-year rate of 35%. They had been relatively isolated from the dotcom boom and bust.

Jim had joined the Marketing department three years earlier as a product manager for one of the products. He had previously been with another small software development house, originally as a software engineer, and then as a product manager. He was relatively quiet, unassuming, a hard worker, and quite creative. Jim was well liked and respected in the company, but not seen as a high flyer.

At an ERP exhibition about two years ago, Jim came across the stand of a company offering a new product or service related to the ASP (Application-Specific Provider) business model. In essence this new model hosted an application for an organization, charging rental fees rather than a license fee. Jim was very excited by this idea, and back in the office the next day he set up a meeting to discuss it with Paul, the Sales VP. Jim didn't get the response he expected or wanted. Paul said he didn't think that Jim's idea would work, as none of his customers had asked for it. Besides, it would take years to develop and he couldn't see any opportunity that year. He suggested that Jim take up the idea with Steve, the VP for R&D. Jim left the meeting downhearted but thought it quite possible that Steve would help. On reflection, he thought he should have set up a meeting with him first. Jim also regretted not having sat down before the meeting to think through his idea, and to anticipate Paul's views. If he had done so, he might have foreseen the eventual outcome.

Before his meeting with Steve, Jim pulled some data off the Web and researched the whole area of ASPs. He also researched the competition, using personal contacts to gauge whether other organizations were planning anything similar. Jim also knew that Steve liked new ideas and thinking and was happy to leap into new developments.

Jim's research produced interesting results: a recently published report from an industry analyst had suggested that ASPs were the next big wave, and he also discovered that none of the competition was doing anything.

Jim put together a small report with outline proposals and sent it to Steve. When they met, Steve said he liked the proposals and had been thinking along similar lines. In fact he had mentioned the idea to Doug, Pluto's President, but had not received much interest. Doug had suggested that it could be something for next year's budget.

Steve and Jim both felt it was an idea worth pursuing, and discussed how they might move forward, although they were cautious about the possible response if they raised it again with the top team. They eventually decided to do a number of things in parallel, and both to work on a projection of potential business.

In doing further research, they looked at the impact this new model might have on their existing revenue streams, the holder of which was the VP for Sales. This might be a big barrier. That set them thinking about other barriers, so they brainstormed a list, of which the main ones were:

» a lack of understanding of the new concept;
» the impact on today's customers, business, and revenues;
» existing R&D projects, having a broad number of opportunities;
» a limited budget within the organization for this kind of work; and
» challenges that the organization was already having with two of its biggest implementations.

Other initiatives they started were:

» to get the ASP company to visit Pluto Inc. and present to them; and
» to look at ways of partnering.

Jim used some of his Marketing budget and Steve some of his Research budget.

Three months later, the challenges that the organization was having with the two implementations created an opportunity. The main problems with the projects were the changing requirements specifications from the clients, poor documentation, slow responses on both sides, and some conflict and confusion on Pluto's side. Both clients were unhappy with progress and were talking about pulling out of the contracts.

Steve suggested that they move to a Rapid Application Development (RAD) approach, using DSDM (Dynamic Systems Development Method) techniques. This approach is based on nine key principles that focus on such things as active user involvement, and for which fitness for business purpose is the essential criterion for acceptance.

Jim recognized that the situation now presented an ideal opportunity to demonstrate the value of a hosted model and driver for the new ASP business model. If they adopted the hosted model, both parties could see in real-time how the application was developing, and either approve or disapprove developments. This would save money and time, and improve communication.

Jim and Steve went back first to Paul, the Sales VP, and then to Doug, the President, to discuss their ideas and proposals and the value that they offered to the current projects.

This time, both parties liked and accepted the ideas, and immediately approved a budget for their implementation. Although this was not what Jim had in mind originally, the concept had developed to its next stage.

That was the good news. However, one of the project managers was very unhappy about the idea. He felt that his team were just getting on top of the issues and slowly resolving the problems, and that this new idea would only add to the difficulties.

A year after these events took place, Steve had left Pluto Inc. to join another organization, but Jim had been promoted to Marketing VP.

So what lessons can be learnt from this case study?

» There are important personal qualities required to be an effective change agent. These include:
  » being persistent and not giving up;
  » being creative enough to find ways around barriers and blocks;
  » understanding the specific reasons why people don't like a particular idea;
  » finding a sponsor;
  » being as specific as possible; and
  » being flexible and responsive, and adapting your ideas and thinking as you go.
» Think about the other people involved or whom you're trying to influence. Analyze and assess:
  » what drives them;
  » what motivates them; and
  » what's in it for them.
» You can never please all of the people all of the time – there will be both "winners" (those impacted positively) and "losers" (those impacted negatively).
» Planning is important.
» Think ahead.
» Anticipate other people's reactions.

» Sell the value to the other parties.
» Decide how you will communicate and position your ideas.
» Find allies - people with similar interests, or to whom you can put a win-win proposition.
» Start with small steps and early wins.

CASE STUDY 2: DAIMLERCHRYSLER

The unfolding story of the merger between Daimler and Chrysler since its announcement in 1998 provides an illuminating insight into a major change program involving every dimension of strategy and change. It is the story of the formation of a global partnership between two very large and very different organizations. The real test was that of turning the idea into a reality; making the change happen is the challenge of OC. This was particularly true in this case, where there were major challenges from the differences between the companies, and in managing the resulting integration and consolidation. The figures involved are awesome - the creation of a company valued at $40bn, with a total of 420,000 employees, making 2.3 million cars a year.

Any initiative on this scale has to be "strategic", i.e. one aimed at the longer term. The question of the timescale on which the success of the merger should be viewed is difficult to answer, but it is likely to be at least a 10-year timeframe. The decision to merge was based on a view of how the industry, customers, and competition will change, and what it will take to compete, survive, and win in the long term. With any plan, its rationale, results, and success will primarily be judged with the benefit of hindsight at some point in the future. This case study includes events up to the middle of 2001.

Mergers are the organizational equivalent of marriages. They have to cope with all the benefits and problems associated with the joining of two entities into what it is hoped will be a lifelong relationship. The trick is moving from the honeymoon phase into making it really work - which requires determination, hard work, and persistence. For it to succeed, the relationship has to meet the goals, aspirations, and styles of both parties. The chairman of the combined company, Jurgen Schrempp, admitted that the task of integrating the people could take up to five years.

At the time of the merger announcement in 1998 there were discussions as to whether it was a true merger, or really a take-over by Daimler. After the merger a joke went round the US asking how you pronounce the name of the German–American car company. The answer was "Daimler", the "Chrysler" being silent!

First let us consider the background to the merger, in the period 1997–8. The main worldwide trends at the forefront of executive minds included:

» globalization – being one of the top three global market leaders, with global scale and reach, and so increasing the consolidation of the big players;
» poor growth prospects; and
» increasing demand for returns from shareholders.

Within the global automotive industry, general opinions at the time of the mid-to-late 1990s recognized:

» the large number of players in the industry;
» the existing domination by the big two of GM and Toyota;
» the considerable over-capacity in production against sales;
» the increasing costs of development – and the need to share risks and costs;
» that lower-range segments are catching up the higher-quality segments in terms of standards and features;
» changing customer requirements – new segments forming or being created, with new products creating and grabbing niche markets such as MPVs (multi-purpose vehicles) and SUVs (sport utility vehicles);
» increasing competition;
» that only the number one and number two companies will be able to compete in the main car markets; and
» the increasing importance of scale and size.

Chrysler had recognized that it was a considerably smaller player, with its main base in the US. It therefore needed a strategy either to increase its size and scale through some form of merger, or to become a niche player. It was very much a mass-market manufacturer at the time. The obvious option was to sell out to Ford or GM.

From Daimler's point of view it also needed to become a global player. Its primary base was in Europe, and it was seen as a high-end-market manufacturer. It therefore needed both to gain a presence in the US and to gain access to a product that was more suitable for the mass market. The obvious choices were to seek a merger, or to acquire a US provider.

Chrysler therefore seemed to be a logical choice for Daimler. There were great opportunities for synergy, most of each organization's operations complementing the other in terms of geography, products, and markets. Table 7.1 demonstrates these synergies.

However, there were real challenges with this merger in a number of areas: culture differences, organizational structures, and merging the operations of the two giant organizations into one whole.

Discussions between the two chairmen, Jurgen Schrempp of Daimler and Bob Easton of Chrysler, started in 1996 and continued into 1997. The boards of the respective organizations were brought into the negotiations in late 1997, and the merger was announced in early 1998 and completed later that year.

As is always the case in a merger, one of the biggest justifications was that major cost reduction could take place as the operations of the two organizations were rationalized. Other sources of savings would derive from their combined purchasing power. Figures of $1.4bn in the first year were forecast, together with $3bn annually after three to five years.

Following the completion of the merger, 12 integration projects were formed. Initial attempts at integrating the two organizations' operations fell into difficulties and it was decided to maintain two parallel organizations – one American and one German. This led to a couple of issues: the reduced scope for the savings that were expected, and the fact that it reinforced the gap between the organizations. At the same time, some key Chrysler executives decided to leave the organization, in part blaming interference and the Teutonic style of management.

Chrysler's operation then started to under-perform badly. This was coupled with the start of a downturn and reduced sales. Profits and the share price of the new organization started dropping considerably. In an attempt to halt the rot, Schrempp decided to appoint a German

Table 7.1 Synergies between Daimler and Chrysler.

Dimension	Daimler–Benz	Chrysler
Company's primary business(es)	Automotive Aerospace	Automotive
Legal entity	German	US
Market segment	Niche-market	Mass-market
Market position in home market	No 2 in home German market of luxury car makers – against BMW	No 3 in the US market, behind Ford and GM in sales
Products	Luxury cars: C class, E class, A class vans, trucks	Vans, work-vehicles SUVs
Brand	High-end, luxury	Rugged, mass-market
Geographic sales market strength	Europe	US
Manufacturing operations	Germany, started in US in 1997	US
Nationality	German/European	American
National culture	Disciplined Traditional	Short-term Individualistic Innovative
Business culture/ management style	Semi-independent organizations Longer-term view "Staid" Banks are seen as partners	Shareholder-value driven Short-term view Dynamic
Corporate culture	Engineering Quality Luxury Traditional	Innovative
Core competencies	Engineering	Cars, niche markets Marketing
Corporate governance	Chairman Two-tier board structure Supervisory board Worker representation at board level	Chairman Board of directors No worker representation
Global revenue	$70bn	$60bn (approx. same as D–B)
Number of staff	300,000	120,000 (half)
Production volume	715,000	1.6 million (double)
Profit margin	*(see comparison . . .)*	Twice that of D–B

executive to head up and run the US operations. There is now talk of substantial job cuts to stem losses. Not surprisingly, morale at Chrysler plants has plummeted. Questions and rumors about what Daimler–Benz will do with Chrysler abound.

In considering this merger, even at a simplistic level, a number of obvious learning points can be derived:

» There is always a challenge in balancing the needs of today's business against working to implement the plans for tomorrow's. The balance is never perfect, but it is important not to lose sight of the current business environment, particularly in crisis situations.

» There is a corresponding risk of the focus of corporate attention switching to internal concerns rather than to the more important external matters of customers, markets, and economics. An organization must keep its eye on the ball.

» An organization's capacity to handle or manage change is finite, limited primarily by resources, a key aspect of which is executive time. This has to be kept in mind in the planning phases, so curbing the usually over-ambitious goals of a change.

» An organization's culture is a very strong part of its make-up. When merging two organizations, their respective cultures must be a key consideration in planning and implementing the change. Too often, the softer elements such as organizational culture are ignored. There are a number of reasons for this: organizational culture is intangible and so cannot be grasped; it is difficult to articulate and so cannot be managed; it is a very strong force and so is difficult to change. To try to change the culture takes a great deal of sustained focus. It is not something that can happen overnight, and in fact takes a significantly longer time than do the other elements.

» Involvement, participation, and consensus at all levels is important, particularly at the top of the organization. However, this has to be balanced with some form of clear directive from above.

» Teamwork is vital, and the need for strong cohesive teams to drive the change is clear. If there is conflict within teams, the change is far more likely to fail. Managing conflict therefore becomes a vital aspect of any change.

» A challenge for change is the paradox of (fast) autocratic change, compared with (slow) participative change. Both styles need to be used, but careful judgements made as to when each is the more appropriate approach in any given situation.

» The people and organizational aspects of any change are as important as the hard financial aspects. One leads to the other. They must be given full attention and consideration in any change, otherwise all will fail.

» Leaders need to act quickly and decisively, as strong leadership is vital in these situations.

» It is vital to be able to understand and quantify the size and amount of change involved. The amount of change and the corresponding time, energy, and resources to manage it are usually underestimated in the planning phase, if a projection is done at all. Typically the perceived amount of change and its actual amount differ by a factor of three or four.

» Finally, personal relationships in any change are very important. Without strong relationships no trust exists. It is well worth investing time and money into developing good relationships. The returns will be great!

CASE STUDY 3: JAPAN

This case study considers a totally different type of OC. It looks at the change of a whole system – a national economy, that of Japan. It considers Japan's economy and all the players within it, including the parties within the Financial and Banking sector, and Government. The dynamics of this scenario mirror many of those found in other contexts and situations, such as when an entire industry undergoes transformation. The case study highlights some factors and issues common to many major transformations, and some of the real challenges that beset change programs. These include:

» the significance of structures and power bases;

» issues arising from the differing and conflicting views and needs of various stakeholder groups;

» the complexity and connectivity of problems and potential solutions;

» the importance of clear leadership;

» the significance of self-perpetuating or self-reinforcing loops;

» the need for new, different, and radical thinking in change situations;

» the need for a clear power base from which to initiate change;
» striking an appropriate balance between short-term and longer-term considerations, acknowledging the risks associated with delay: at best the problems remain static, and at worst they get more difficult as time passes; and
» sources of resistance to change and the difficulties of changing the status quo.

It is these factors that are the key to any change and that, if not addressed, can paralyze a situation, as this case study will demonstrate.

Throughout the 1980s the Japanese economy was booming. Japanese banks were lending increasing amounts of money to companies, but with decreasing levels of security. As the boom turned to bust in 1989, the bad debts started to become apparent. The banks were owed trillions of yen as organizations went bankrupt. The Government, banks, corporations, and the Japanese people have still not recovered.

Since then, over 10 years ago, the Japanese economy has been in the doldrums and beset by the problems caused in the boom. Various attempts to address the fundamental issues have been made, but with limited success. As we look back on these, it is obvious that there are some deeply rooted causes of this malaise that are impeding any potential transformation:

» the situation itself;
» the Japanese culture;
» the parties involved and the structure in which they operate; and
» other factors.

We shall consider each of these in turn.

The situation itself

The financial situation in Japan is very dire. There are a number of deep and fundamental issues with its current economy, the main one being the vast amount of debt currently within the system, owned by banks and corporations. This runs into trillions of yen, and is going to take time to work through. There is only so much that anyone can do to alleviate a problem of this magnitude.

The Japanese culture

This is one of the root causes of the whole situation, contributing to Japan's inability to escape out of its mess. Generalizing, it can be said that the national traits or characteristics of the Japanese people can be described as follows:

» They value consensus rather than firm, clear, strong leadership and direction.
» People are respectful, feeling a pressure to respect and bow to a superior's wisdom and authority, rather than being able to question and challenge issues and decisions.
» Promotion owes more to age than to ability.
» There is great concern to avoid any personal loss of face.
» There is a general pressure to conform to national norms.
» Very few speak openly of difficult issues or advocate criticism; confrontation is definitely not a style that is used.
» The national policy of "lifetime employment" has been a key factor in restraining a company's ability to cut costs. Some of the more enlightened companies are now ditching this type of policy.
» There is a powerful national orientation to protectionism, which has led to the perpetuation of old and inefficient systems. Reform has been sidelined and market forces are not the driving agents for change that they are in other markets. This has exacerbated the problems elsewhere in the country.

The parties involved and the structure in which they operate

Each of the main parties is defined in the systems map in Fig. 7.1. At a macro-level view it describes the structure of "the Japanese system".

Of course, even the Japanese economy does not operate in isolation. It operates in a clear global economy, with truly global markets. So, for example, capital will flow to where there is a perceived maximum return for minimum risk.

Other factors

A number of other factors influence the situation. The first is Japan's political system. The main political party, the LDP (Liberal Democratic

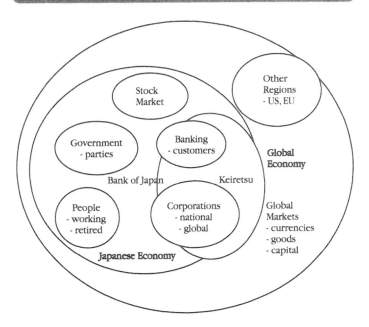

Fig. 7.1 A macro-level map of the Japanese system.

Party), has been in power for most of the past 10 years. Its key supporters are the majority of Japanese people who live in rural areas, who have more to lose under reform, and who thus prefer the status quo, no matter how painful it might be. Elections have resulted in no clear majority for any party, and so there is no clear mandate, with the primary party having to form coalitions to survive and govern. The quality of political leadership, until the recent appointment of Mr Koizumi, was very poor.

There are various powerful Government agencies such as the Ministry of Finance, the Ministry of Trade and Industry, and the Bank of Japan. Without strong political leadership these institutions have devised their own strategies for reform and have acted in isolation, invariably ensuring that their reforms maintain their own vested interests. The result is an emphasis on the short term, aiming for quick wins so that their instigators can be re-elected or re-appointed next time. As a result of the frequent changes in leadership, Government policy has swayed from one approach to another. There have been 13 emergency packages over the past seven years.

Another key factor has been the Japanese banking and financial system. Japanese banks were probably the most guilty of all parties in promoting and leading the boom phase. Figures published in May 2001 suggested that Japanese banks had Yen 80bn of bad loans. The banks and financial institutions have largely attempted to cover up the size of the problem, thereby conveying a sense of denial.

The Keiretsu is a network of formal associations between members of banks and corporations. Large corporations have historically each been allied to a particular bank. Any particular bank is therefore allied to a set of corporations, each member of which has a range of cross-holdings in the shares of other members. There is considerable cross-ownership between the banks and the corporations. In easy times this is a real asset and strength, but it has its downside in more desperate times – this inter-linking and cross-interest has proved to be a block to reform and change as each party seeks to protect its own vested interests and those of its allies.

The Japanese corporations constitute another factor. A degree of secrecy still hangs over the operations of corporations when compared with Western organizations. Historically they have been protected and supported by the Japanese financial system to avoid bankruptcies, although these have now begun to occur.

Various measures and initiatives over the past 10 years have attempted to resolve the situation, but have proved largely unsuccessful. They have suffered from a lack of committed support, caused in part by disagreement over which would be the best and most effective policies.

This case study demonstrates a number of points about the planning and implementation of change in organizations and systems:

» Even when there is a major, recognized "burning platform," there are still substantial barriers to achieving any change, including:
  » the influence of history;
  » the influence of "structures," and their interdependencies;

- » the influence of culture, either national or corporate;
- » the influence of vested interests, at the expense of the greater good; and
- » the influence of power bases.
» Clear and strong personal leadership is needed.
» A compelling vision for the future is required in order to drive action.
» Finding a center path can be a challenge if there is a wide range of constituencies, groups, segments, and stakeholders.
» It is easier to take no decision than to make tough ones.
» Consensus is an important factor.
» It must be accepted that there will be losers in any change.
» Creating and implementing solutions can be difficult.
» There is a need for ideas, new thinking, and solutions in order to bring disparate groups together and to get agreement, decisions, and approval.
» People must be empowered.
» Change is, at the end of the day, about power – and about having more power than that which maintains the status quo.

Key Concepts and Thinkers

» A number of important concepts are useful in OC.
» Certain key thinkers have contributed to the field, and many are still involved.

"The only competitive advantage the company of the future will have is its managers' ability to learn faster than their competitors."

Arie de Geus

This chapter builds on Chapter 6, which outlined the state of the art and included some useful conceptual frameworks. It is divided into two main sections. The first provides an A to Z of key concepts fundamental to the planning and execution of an organizational change (OC). The second introduces the key thinkers and leaders who have had a major influence on the field. Using these concepts, Chapter 10 puts forward a simple but effective ten-step plan to making OC work.

AN A–Z OF KEY TERMS AND CONCEPTS

In selecting which concepts to include, the focus has been on those concepts that help make change work and happen.

(The) Amount of change

When planning any change, the first step is to try to define its planned end-point, and then the size of the change – how much change is involved. This estimating step is absolutely vital, and is more of an art than a science. Things that can help in this respect include the change frameworks or elements (see later in this section). The trick is to be as articulate as possible about what has to change, and to be able to assess how easy or difficult (how resource-intensive) that change will be. Invariably in the planning process the amount of change is underestimated, either by not considering some elements or by not fully recognizing the size of the change.

Barriers and blockers

These are people or things (but ultimately people) who resist, inhibit, or prevent change. They can range from a lack of money, strong power bases, vested interests, not enough "pain", disagreement over what to do or how to respond, or a lack of knowledge and understanding about the change.

Branding and marketing

It is vital to brand any change project or initiative – i.e. to give it a unique identity with which people can associate the change. It is just one element of a marketing strategy and an integral part of the communications strategy for the change. This is all connected to the positioning, profile, and identity of the change. The main objectives are to raise awareness and to gain momentum for the change program.

Buy-in, commitment and ownership

The success of any change can be attributed solely to the extent to which individuals and teams are committed to a particular change or course of action – denoted either by the number of people involved, or by the level of motivation and action focused on the change. Issues for the leadership team include how buy-in and commitment can be achieved, and how responsibility for the change can be owned as far as is possible by those involved.

Cause and effect

A simple but very powerful principle of systems, or systemic, thinking is that of cause and effect. In all situations, but particularly in change situations, knowledge and understanding of the dynamics of cause and effect are very important. For instance, what is driving events, actions, or behavior (the causes)? What impact are certain actions and events having (the effects)? In many situations, certainly when trying to exert an influence, it is convenient for people to attribute a certain effect to one particular cause. In most cases a single causal link to an effect is unlikely – typically there are several causes or influences that result in a particular event.

Change drivers

These are the forces driving a situation that creates a need for change, such as reduced profitability or a new competitor.

Change levers

In any change one has to consider what the key levers are for change. These are not the same as the change drivers. Change levers, as the name suggests, are those elements that will influence the change in the direction you want it to go. There are many change levers that could be used. These include incentives and rewards such as money or promotion, coercion through threats or punishment, communication training and education, and executive support and commitment.

Communication and dialogue

It is imperative in any change that communication – discussion and dialogue – takes place between all parties. There are four main points to bear in mind in any communication:

» decide what you are trying to achieve in the communication;
» identify your target audience(s);
» understand the mindset of those to whom you are trying to communicate; and
» bear in mind that it is not what is transmitted, but what is received and interpreted, that is important.

Constituencies and stakeholders

The importance of "stakeholder management" is absolutely critical. Assessing the main stakeholders is paramount, not only in the planning phase, but also by monitoring their opinions as the change is implemented. Each individual stakeholder will have a different perspective and opinion on the change. It is important to know these views and to deal with them as far as possible. It is useful to categorize stakeholders in various ways – for instance, under common interests, or those for and against, or winners and losers, or into those who express their views and opinions and those who keep quiet.

Critical mass

This concept is linked to the forces and levers driving the change. A change process has achieved a critical mass when the forces working for the change are greater than those against it or neutral about it. A critical phase in the early part of a change is to build a critical mass amongst those involved that will drive the momentum and pressure for the change to take place.

Culture

Culture has been defined in a number of areas in this book. There are many dimensions to it – change culture, the culture that an organization has, measurement of the change, and more. There are positive (enabling) and negative (blocking) aspects of an organization's culture.

Discretionary effort

This is a term that focuses on the extent of commitment to the project. The people involved have varying degrees of commitment to it, reflected in the degree of energy and effort that participants invest. Most of this energy is generally discretionary effort - above and beyond the call of duty, the "extra mile" taken in order to meet the program's goals.

FUD – Fear, uncertainty and doubt

This concept relates to the more emotional responses to change, or to a strategy adopted by those against the change. They may create and disseminate any amount of misinformation to support their cause. This was certainly true in the days when BPR was in vogue, and people feared losing their jobs because of the fashion of downsizing.

Hearts and minds

This notion is fundamental to both change and leadership. It is vital to be able to influence and communicate with people on both a rational and an emotional level. A point to note is that at a personal level most people react initially to change emotionally, and then switch to a more rational response. The importance and difficulty of winning hearts and minds in change situations cannot be overestimated.

Inertia

People and organizations undergoing change have a high degree of inertia, or difficulty of moving from their current positions. (The term comes from the field of physics.) This is a very powerful factor and should never be underestimated when planning any change. Levers to counter this include communication, education, a compelling reason to change, "WIIFM" (What's In It For Me - see later in this section), and involvement or empowerment. It takes a lot of time and energy to get momentum going in the first place.

Internalization

This refers to the process in which a person starts to internalize aspects of the program, whether by different behavior, by new attitudes, or through new ways of working. It develops as an individual recognizes and believes that this change is important, is useful or that there is no other option. This comes as a result of communication, training, or other levers of change. It is a key part of the change cycle for people. Once internalization starts to take place, leaders and managers know that the change has started to take effect, and that half of the battle to win people's hearts and minds has been won.

Language and symbolism

Language and symbols are central to any change. Both send very important messages to the intended audience. However, the real issue is how these messages are interpreted. This interpretation process depends upon the receiver's individual filters and perceptions. The interpretation of any key message is very dependent on the type of language used. Too much "management speak" is derided. There are a number of issues with communications about change:

» In any change it is important to create and maintain a common and consistent language associated with it. This gives people a common framework, a link to the change, and a common understanding, a "new" language that helps with the element of compelling vision.
» Language can be divisive, perhaps through unwise use of jargon, or between people with different aptitudes, or between those not in the same league, or between groups not having the same level of knowledge, such as between general staff and management or those with MBAs.
» The symbolic effect of language and its impact on others should be recognized, especially when attempting to communicate across boundaries and interfaces.

(The) Long March

This alludes to the recognition that change does not happen overnight and that there is no such thing as a quick fix. Change can be a long process, requiring sustained energy and commitment. The term relates to the amount of attention or time that any particular stakeholder will give to the change in which you are involved. In an ideal situation, executives totally committed to a change project should give as much attention as the project team requires throughout the life of the program. Typically, however, after the initial promotion of the launch a very common trend is that interest and commitment soon wane, overtaken by other and newer campaigns.

Power

Power, both formal and informal, is important in any change. It is needed to overcome the resistance of moving away from the status quo. Change is in essence a battle – the military connotation is clear. There are many forms and sources of power. Formal sources include money, seniority, role, title, status, level, and information. Informal sources include people – their time and energy, personal power, credibility, knowledge, experience, style, and ideas.

Quick wins

Change will not happen unless there are very good reasons for it to do so. There need to be good reasons and justifications to support it, and evidence of benefits – particularly at the early stages. This can be achieved through deliberately targeting and realizing some quick wins, especially early on. This enables positive messages to be transmitted, and helps in the battle to gain commitment and to demonstrate results and value.

Sacred cows

In any organization there are always some elements, usually not spoken about, that everyone knows are non-negotiable – for instance, "Market share is our number one priority", or "We have always sold direct", or "A&B have always been our ad agency". They also share the characteristic that they are usually hidden assumptions. In a change process they need to be brought to the surface and made visible, and their implications reviewed. Any change usually involves killing a few sacred cows.

Sphere of influence

This concept is another key one for people involved in change. It relates to the power someone has over the people around him or her.

It is fairly subjective, and has little to do with formal hierarchy and status. Change agents need to maximize their spheres of influence. It is interesting to note that a person's sphere of influence is *always* much greater than the individual believes it to be.

States

Beckhard and Harris (see Chapter 6 and the next section of this chapter) wrote a seminal work on OC, identifying the three main states of change as the "as is", the "to be", and the "transition state". The definition of each of these three states is important when managing change. Certainly the more the "to be" state can be defined, the easier it will be to manage the change. The other key point here is the significance of the transition state. Transitions are always the most difficult to make, and the state between the start and end points of a change is a critical issue.

(The) Status quo

This is the position before any change project, representing the environment as it is today. The whole point of a change is to alter the existing balance or status quo – this will probably include changes to the structure, processes, and behavior of an organization or team. Usually the biggest source of resistance comes from those who either have something to lose or fear the proposed change.

Unintended, unanticipated and unexpected outcomes

In any change, not everything goes perfectly or as anticipated. Unexpected situations often arise. Examples abound, especially around new performance metrics where creative employees always find ways around the system. It is important that some consideration is given in the planning phase to "what ifs". Tactics to ensure that these surprises are kept to a minimum include regular staff surveys and pilot programs.

Vested interests

It is a truism that individuals, particularly at a more senior level, either have more to gain or have more to lose from any particular change. These vested interests are important in assessing an individual's response to a change.

Views from different heights or levels

This simple and obvious concept refers to the fact that people at different levels in an organization or project see the world very differently. This important fact has a profound impact on the potential areas of disagreement and conflict that may occur in a project. There are a number of very good reasons for these differences in perception, primary amongst which are differences in the roles, responsibilities, and information available at each level.

WIIFM (What's in it for me)

A key practical consideration for any of the stakeholders in a change project is "So what's in it for me?". This can be either an overt or a covert influence on how people view any particular change. However, ignore this at your peril when considering or planning any change.

KEY THINKERS

This section identifies the key leaders of thinking in the field of OC. This material is developed in Chapter 9, which lists resources, many pertaining to these thinkers, academics, and writers. As there are so many who could be mentioned, some restriction has had to be made.

Kurt Lewin

Kurt Lewin was one of the founding fathers of the field of OC. His background was in psychology and some of his early work in the late 1940s focused on group dynamics. He will be forever known as the founder of force field analysis, which treats an existing status quo as being pushed from one side by forces driving change, and from the other by forces resisting it. The other work for which Lewin is famous is his process model for change, consisting of three phases:

1 unfreeze;
2 change; and
3 re-freeze.

Details of his work are outlined in Chapter 9.

Warren Bennis

Warren Bennis was an early writer on change and leadership, writing his first book, *The Planning of Change*, in 1962. He has been a prolific author, with a range of substantial texts on both subjects. He is an academic, holding the position of Professor of Management at the University of Southern California. One of Bennis's recurring themes is that of the leader as social architect. He identified four core competencies or abilities for leaders: those of managing attention, meaning, trust, and self.

John Kotter

John Kotter, a Professor at Harvard Business School, is probably one of the best-known writers on the subject of organizational change. Interestingly, his real specialty concerns leadership, but of course this is a central and integral component of change. His most famous piece of work is the eight steps to a successful organizational transformation, described in Chapter 6. His seminal work is the book *Leading Change* (details of which are in Chapter 9), although he has written many other books on the subject of leadership.

Rosabeth Moss Kanter

Rosabeth Moss Kanter, currently a Professor at Harvard, has had a distinguished career in the academic field and is a leading authority in the field of managing change. Her background was in sociology and this shows in her writing and interpretation of change. She has written many books on the subject, focusing on the wider change implications for the "post-entrepreneurial" organization. These are outlined in Chapter 9.

Jeannie Daniel Duck

Jeannie Daniel Duck is an experienced change consultant, working for the Boston Consulting Group. She has written a number of articles and books on the subject. In a *Harvard Business Review* article entitled "The art of balancing", she proposes that leaders of change need to take a holistic and connected approach to change rather than the reductionist approach taken until now. She has recently written a book looking at the challenges of OC, called *The Change Monster: the human forces that fuel or foil corporate transformation and change*.

Daryl Conner

In the 1970s Daryl Conner formed what was probably the first change consulting company. He developed a lot of the practical tools, concepts and techniques that now form the basic approaches to OC used by many organizations and consultancies. He has written several books on the subject, as described in Chapter 9.

Richard Beckhard

Richard Beckhard was a prominent leader of thinking in the field of OC in the late 1970s, and co-authored a number of seminal books on the subject. Probably the most important idea that he developed was that of the transition state in OC.

Peter Senge

Peter Senge is Director of the Systems Thinking and Organizational Learning Program at the Sloan School of Management, MIT. He has written a number of books relevant to OC, including *The Fifth Discipline*, which focuses on systems thinking and organizational learning, and *The Dance of Change*, which focuses on the challenges of sustaining momentum in learning organizations.

Gary Hamel

Gary Hamel is Professor of Strategic and International Management at the London Business School and founder and chairman of Strategos. His interest is strategy and he has written a number of books on business strategy in conjunction with other authors such as C.K. Prahalad, with whom he wrote *Competing for the Future* and other titles. In his own recent book *Leading the Revolution*, he calls for a radical re-think and transformation concerning how individuals and organizations view the future. This is a rather personal view on the transitions taking place in the world's organizations and their impact on individuals. He stresses that the old types of change characterized by incremental improvements are now defunct and that the only way forward is radical change, led by radical change agents at all levels in the organization.

Tom Peters

Tom Peters co-wrote the classic book *In Search of Excellence* in 1982 with Robert Waterman. They were then both consultants at McKinsey. Peters went on to write *Thriving on Chaos* in 1987 and *Liberation Management* in 1992.

Edgar Schein

Schein is currently a Professor at the Sloan School of Management, MIT. His background is as a social psychologist. He has written on many subjects, amongst them leadership, motivation, and culture. He expressed the view that the key to successful leadership was managing culture change in an organization. He is probably a man ahead of his time in terms of his thinking and ideas. His recent works have focused on the cultural aspects of organizations, defining culture as "what is learned as a total social unit over the course of its history". He also believes passionately in the need for consensus as a key part of any OC.

Resources

» There are a multitude of resources, including books, business and academic journals, and the Web. This chapter provides many examples.

"You can take a horse to water, but you can't make him drink."

This book may have provoked you into feeling you don't know enough about the subject of organizational change (OC), made you hungry for more, and inspired you to go and learn far more about the subject than can be covered here in just 30,000 words. If this has been its effect, then this chapter holds information on what to do and where to go next. There is a wide range of information and reading on the subject, from books and journals through to some interesting Websites.

BOOKS FROM PRACTITIONERS AND BUSINESS LEADERS

» Jan Carlzon, the man who ran and turned around the Scandinavian Airlines System (SAS) in the mid-1980s, wrote *Moments of Truth* (Harper Perennial, ISBN 0 06 091580 3).
» Sir John Harvey-Jones, the man who turned around UK chemical giant ICI in the 1980s and then turned business guru in the BBC series *Troubleshooter*, wrote *Making it Happen* (Fontana, ISBN 0 00 637409 3).
» Andrew Pettigrew, one-time CEO of ICI, wrote *The Awakening Giant: continuity & change in ICI* (Blackwell, ISBN 0 631 134557).
» Jack Welch, often described as the best modern business leader, has co-written numerous books on his successes and his approach. Two of them, with co-author Robert Slater, are *Jack Welch & the GE Way* (McGraw-Hill, ISBN 0 07 058104 5) and *The GE Way Fieldbook* (McGraw-Hill, ISBN 0 07 135481 6).
» Sony's co-founder, the late Akio Morita, wrote *Made in Japan* (Fontana, ISBN 0 00 637234 1).
» The turnaround of the American car giant Chrysler in the mid-1970s by Lee Iacocca is documented in *Iacocca: an autobiography* (Bantam Books, ISBN 0 55 325147 3).
» The turnaround of IBM in the mid-1990s following its biggest single loss in a year of $5bn has been written up by journalist Doug Garr in *IBM Redux: Lou Gerstner & the business turnaround of the decade* (Harper Collins, ISBN 0 887 30944 5).

» David Greising, author and journalist, has written the story of Roberto Goizueta, who headed up Coca-Cola, in *I'd Like the World to Buy a Coke: The life and leadership of Roberto Goizueta* (John Wiley & Sons, ISBN 0 471 34594 6).

» The story of the US airline start-up Southwest Airlines is told by Kevin and Jackie Freiberg and Tom Peters in *Nuts! Southwest Airlines' Crazy Recipe for Business Success* (Texere Publishing, ISBN 0 75281334 X).

» Lastly, two books drawing lessons from an earlier age: Donald G. Krause *The Art of War for Executives* (Perigree Books, ISBN 0 399 51902 5), which relates to Sun Tzu's classic work *The Art of War*; and Niccolo Machiavelli *The Prince* (Penguin, ISBN 0 14 044752 0).

BOOKS OUTLINING ACADEMIC IDEAS AND THEORY

There are a few books on best practice, including:

» From the PricewaterhouseCoopers Change Integration Team:
  » *Better Change: Best practice for transforming your organization* (McGraw-Hill, ISBN 0 7863 0342 5); and
  » *The Paradox Principles: How high performing companies manage chaos, complexity, and contradiction to achieve superior results* (PWC-Irwin, ISBN 0 7863 04995)
» A study from Business Intelligence: *Managing and Sustaining Radical Change* (ISBN 1 898 085 26 9).

There are a number of books that summarize the field of OC, including two from Harvard Business School Publishing (HBSP): *Harvard Business Review on Change* (ISBN 0 87584 884 2) and *Harvard Business Review on Managing Uncertainty* (ISBN 0 87584 908 3).

Many leading thinkers in the field have written excellent articles in periodicals and journals (some of the classic ones are listed later in this chapter). Books by them include:

» Julia Balogun & Veronica Hope-Hailey: *Exploring Corporate Strategy* (FT/Prentice Hall, ISBN 0 13 263856 8);

» Richard Beckhard & Reuben Harris: *Organizational Transitions: Managing complex change* (Addison-Wesley, ISBN 0 201 10887 9);

» Richard Beckhard & Wendy Pritchard: *Changing the Essence* (Jossey-Bass, ISBN 1 55542412 0);

» William Bridges: *Managing Transitions* (Perseus Press, ISBN 1 85788 112 5);

» Peter Checkland: *Systems Thinking, Systems Practice: includes a 30-year retrospective* (John Wiley & Sons, ISBN 0 471 98606 2); and *Soft Systems Methodology* (John Wiley & Sons)

» Clayton Christensen: *The Innovator's Dilemma* (Harper Business, ISBN 0 06662 069 4);

» James Collins & Jerry Porras: *Built to Last* (Harper Business, ISBN 0 88730 671 3);

» Daryl Conner: *Managing at the Speed of Change* (Villard, ISBN 0 679 40684 0) and *Leading at the Edge of Chaos* (John Wiley & Sons, ISBN 0 471 29557 4);

» Robert Fritz: *Corporate Tides* (Butterworth-Heinemann, ISBN 0 7506 2149 4);

» Gary Hamel, C.K. Prahalad, Howard Thomas & Don O'Neal (editors): *Strategic Flexibility: Managing in a turbulent environment* (John Wiley & Sons, ISBN 0 471 984 736);

» Charles Handy: *The Empty Raincoat* (Hutchinson, ISBN 0 09 178022 5) and *The Age of Unreason* (Arrow Books, ISBN 0 09 975740);

» Rosabeth Moss Kanter: *The Change Masters* (George Allen & Unwin, ISBN 0 04 658241 X), *When Giants Learn to Dance* (HBSP), *The Challenge of Organizational Change*, and recently *eVolve!* (HBSP, ISBN 1 57851 439 8);

» Jon Katzenbach: *Real Change Leaders* (Nicholas Brealey, ISBN 1 85788 1508);

» John Kotter: *Leading Change* (HBSP, ISBN 0 875 847471);

» Eddie Obeng: *All Change: The project leader's secret handbook* (FT/Prentice Hall, ISBN 0 273 62221 8) and *Putting Strategy to Work* (FT/Prentice Hall, ISBN 0 273 602659);

» James O'Toole: *Leading Change* (Jossey-Bass, ISBN 1 55542 608 5);

» Peter Senge: *The Fifth Discipline* (Doubleday, ISBN 0 385 26094 6) and *The Dance of Change* (Doubleday, ISBN 0 385 49322 3); and

» Douglas K. Smith: *Taking Charge of Change* (Perseus Books, ISBN 0 201 91604 5).

JOURNALS AND PERIODICALS

There are a range of academic journals and periodicals containing material on OC. Some are more focused on the subject than others, and some are more academic than others. The main ones are listed below:

» *Academy of Management Journal*
» *Academy of Management Review*
» *Administrative Science Quarterly*
» *California Management Review*
» *Harvard Business Review (HBR)*
» *Journal of Applied Behavioral Science*
» *Journal of Change Management*
» *Journal of General Management*
» *Journal of Management Consultants*
» *Journal of Management Studies*
» *Journal of Organizational Behavior*
» *Journal of Strategic Change*
» *Long Range Planning* (published by the Strategic Planning Society)
» *Management Review*
» *McKinsey Quarterly*
» *Organisational Dynamics*
» *Organization Studies*
» *Sloan Management Review*
» *Strategic Management Journal*
» *Fast Company*: www.fastcompany.com

Table 9.1 contains a selection of the best articles relating to organizational change in academic periodicals and journals.

Table 9.1 A selection of articles in academic periodicals and journals.

Title	Author(s)	Publisher
1979		
Choosing strategies for change	J. Kotter & L. Schlesinger	*HBR*, Mar – Apr
1980		
A model for diagnosing organizations	D. Nadler & M. Tushman	*Organisational Dynamics*, Autumn
Managing strategic change	J. Quinn	*Sloan Management Review* Vol 21, No 4
1982		
OD & change	C. Faucheux, G. Amado & A. Laurent	*Annual Review of Psychology* Vol 33
Evolution & revolution – a quantum view of structural change in organizations	D. Miller	*Journal of Management Studies*
Managing transitions to uncertain future states	D. Nadler	*Organisational Dynamics*, Summer
Transition management: an in-depth look at managing complex change	L. Ackerman	*Organisational Dynamics*, Summer
OC techniques: their present & future	S. Michael	*Organisational Dynamics*, Summer
Managing change strategically – the technical, political, and cultural keys	N. Tichy	*Organisational Dynamics*, Autumn
Transforming organizations: the key to strategy is context	S. Davis	*Organisational Dynamics*, Winter
1984		
The leadership challenge: a call for transformational leaders	N. Tichy & D. Ulrich	*Sloan Management Review* Vol 25, No 1
Coming to a new awareness of organizational culture	E. Schein	*Sloan Management Review* Vol 25, No 2, 3–16

Table 9.1 (*Continued*).

Title	Author(s)	Publisher
1985		
How to implement radical strategies in large organizations	Y. Allaire & M. Firsirotu	*Sloan Management Review* Vol 26, No 3, Spring
Organizational evolution - a metamorphosis model of convergence & reorientation	M. Tushman & E. Romanelli	*Journal of Organizational Behavior* Vol 7
1986		
Convergence & upheaval: managing the unsteady pace of organizational evolution	M. Tushman, W. Newman & E. Romanelli	*California Management Review* Vol 29, 29–44
Managing culture: the invisible barrier to strategic change	J. Lorsch	*California Management Review* Vol 28, No 2, Winter, 95–109
Second-order planned change: definition and conceptualization	A. Levy	*Organisational Dynamics* Vol 15, No 1, Summer, 5–20
1987		
Organizational transformations - periodicity & dynamics	Various	*Journal of Management Studies*, Nov, Special issue
The creation of momentum for change through the process of strategic issue diagnosis	J. Dutton & R. Duncan	*Strategic Management Journal* Vol 8, No 3, May – June
1988		
Can change in organizational culture really be managed?	T. Fitzgerald	*Organisational Dynamics*, Autumn
Transformational & coercive strategies for planned OC: beyond the OD model	D. Dunphy & D. Stace	*Organization Studies* Vol 9, No 3, 317–34

(*Continued overleaf*)

Table 9.1 (*Continued*).

Title	Author(s)	Publisher
1989		
Making fast strategic decisions in high velocity environments	K. Eisenhardt	*Academy of Management Journal* Vol 32, No 3
Strategic change: the effects of founding & history	W. Boeker	*Academy of Management Journal* Vol 32, No 3
Organizational framebending: principles for management orientation	D. Nadler & M. Tushman	*Academy of Management Journal* Vol 3
1990		
Why change programs don't produce change	M. Beer, R. Eisenstat & B. Spector	*HBR*, Nov – Dec
Beyond the charismatic leader: leadership & OC	D. Nadler & M. Tushman	*California Management Review*, Winter
1991		
Organizational inertia and momentum: a dynamic model of strategic change	D. Kelly & T. Amburgey	*Academy of Management Journal* Vol 34, No 3
Revolutionary change theories: a multi-level exploration of the punctuated equilibrium paradigm	C.J.G. Gersick	*Academy of Management Review* Vol 16, No 1
Creating successful organization change	L. Goodstein & W.W. Burke	*Organisational Dynamics* Vol 19, No 4
1992		
Why operations improvement programs fail	R.S. Kaufman	*Sloan Management Review*, 34
Successful change programs begin with results	R. Schaffer & H. Thompson	*HBR*, Jan – Feb

Table 9.1 (*Continued*).

Title	Author(s)	Publisher
1993		
Managing change	J. Duck	*HBR*, Nov – Dec
The re-invention roller coaster	T. Goss, R. Pascale & A. Athos	*HBR*, Nov – Dec
Changing the mind of the corporation	R. Martin	*HBR*, Nov – Dec
1994		
How multinational CEOs make change programs stick	B. Bertsch & R Williams	*Long Range Planning* Vol 27, Oct
Integrative management in a time of transformation	K. Bleicher	*Long Range Planning* Vol 27, Oct
Managing strategic evolution in fast-paced technical environments – the case of software development in Silicon Prairie	M. Levenhagen & J. Porac	*Journal of Strategic Change* Vol 5, No 5, Sept – Oct
Chaos theory & strategy: theory, application & managerial implications	D. Levy	*Strategic Management Journal* Vol 15
1995		
Hurdle the cross-functional barriers to strategic change	M.D. Hutt, B.A. Walker & G.L. Franwick	*Sloan Management Review*, Spring
Explaining development & change in organizations	A. Van de Ven M.S. Poole	*Academy of Management Review* Vol 20, No 3
Process strategies for turnaround change agents	A. Armenakis & W.D. Fredenberger	*Journal of Strategic Change* Vol 4, No 1, Jan – Feb
Designing change programs that won't cost you your job	R. Dickhout M. Denham N. Blackwell	*McKinsey Quarterly* No 4
Reengineering – a light that failed?	J. Champy	*Across the Board* Vol 32, No 3, Mar

(*Continued overleaf*)

Table 9.1 *(Continued).*

Title	Author(s)	Publisher
Why transformation efforts fail	J. Kotter	*HBR*, Mar – Apr
1996		
Why do employees resist change? *(Philips case study)*	P. Strebel	*HBR*, May – June
Reaching & changing front-line employees	T. Larkin & S. Larkin	*HBR*, May – June
Strategy as revolution	G. Hamel	*HBR*, July – Aug
The ambidextrous organization: managing evolutionary and revolutionary change	M. Tushman & C. O'Reilly III	*California Management Review*, Summer
1997		
The matrix of change	E. Brynjolfsson, A. Renshaw & M. van Alstyne	*Sloan Management Review*, Winter
An improvisational model for change management: the case of groupware technologies	W.J. Orlikowski & J.D. Hofman	*Sloan Management Review*, Winter, "Change" special issue
A new strategy framework for coping with turbulence	B. Chakravarthy	*Sloan Management Review*, Winter
The paradoxes of new managers as levers of OC	A. Rieple	*Strategic Change* Vol 6, No 4, July
Accelerating strategic change	T. Grundy	*Strategic Change* Vol 6, No 1, Jan – Feb
Igniting OC from below – the power of personal initiative	A. Frohman	*Organisational Dynamics*, Winter
Strategy at the edge of chaos	E. Beinhocker	*McKinsey Quarterly*, No 1
Changing the way we change	R. Pascale, M. Millemann & L. Gioja	*HBR*, Nov – Dec

Table 9.1 (*Continued*).

Title	Author(s)	Publisher
1998		
Employee involvement & the middle managers	M. Fenton-O'Creery	*Journal of Organizational Behavior* Vol 19, No 1, Jan
Focusing strategic change to maximize business performance	J. Wilson	*Strategic Change* Vol 7, No 6, Sept – Oct
Leverage, resistance & the success of implementation approaches	P. Nutt	*Journal of Management Studies* Vol 35, No 2, Mar
Strategy implementation – the new realities	P. Lorange	*Long Range Planning* Vol 31, No 1
Transformational leadership	G. Dess, J. Picken & D. Lyon	*Long Range Planning* Vol 31, No 5
Competing on the edge of chaos	K. Eisenhardt & S. Brown	*Long Range Planning* Vol 31, No 5, issue on "Strategy at the leading edge"
1999		
The organization of the future – principles of design for the 21st Century	D. Nadler & M. Tushman	*Organisational Dynamics*, Summer
Implementing organizational change projects – impediments & gaps	S. Cicmil	*Strategic Change* Vol 8, No 2, Mar – Apr
OD & change – the legacy of the 90s	D. Buchanan, T. Claydon & M. Doyle	*Human Resources Management Journal* Vol 9 No 2
Taking charge at work: extra-role efforts to initiate workplace change	E. Morrison & C. Philips	*Academy of Management Journal* Vol 42, No 4

(*Continued overleaf*)

Table 9.1 (*Continued*).

Title	Author(s)	Publisher
Building a company on Internet time – lessons from Netscape	D. Yoffle & M. Cusumano	*California Management Review* Vol 41, No 3, Spring
2000		
Strategy as guided evolution	B. Lovas & C. S. Ghoshal	*Strategic Management Journal* Vol 21, No 9, Sept
Putting metaphors to work for change in organizations	G. Akin & I. Palmer	*Organisational Dynamics*
Meeting the challenge of disruptive change	C. Christiensen M. Overdorf	*HBR*, Mar – Apr
2001		
The courage to act – what it takes to execute new business strategies	M. Klein & R. Napier	*Journal of Change Management*, Vol 1, No 3, Feb

WEBSITES

Consultancies

» **Andersen Consulting Services**: www.ac.com/services/ebs/tools/ebs_tools2.html
» **Boston Consulting Group's Organization Practice**: www.bcg.com/practice/organization.asp
» **LaMarsh and Associates**: www.lamarsh.com
» **McKinsey**: www.mckinsey.com (search on "change management")
» **Metrus Group**: www.metrus.com
» **ODR**: www.odrinc.com
» **PricewaterhouseCoopers**: pwcglobal.com
» **Pritchett, LLC**: www.pritchettnet.com

Education and training

» **HBR (Harvard Business Review) / HBSP (Harvard Business School Publishing)**: www.hbsp.harvard.edu

» **Pentacle (Eddie Obeng's Virtual Business School)**: www.pentaclethevbs.com

Best practice
» **European Foundation for Quality Management**: www.efqm.org
» **Investors in People Standard**: www.iipuk.co.uk
» **Malcolm Baldridge Awards**: www.quality.nist.gov
» **Project Management Institute**: www.pmi.org
» **Quality Tools Guide**: www.ifigure.com/qual

General information
» **Change Management Resource Library**: www.change-management.org
» **Options for Change**: www.optionsfc.com
» **Organizational Development Toolpack**: www.toolpack.com
» **Society for Organizational Learning**: www.solonline.org
» **Soundview Executive Book Summaries**: www.summaries.com
» **Systems Thinking Practice**: www.sgzz.ch/links/stp
» **General Electric**: www.ge.com
» **Dilbert**: www.dilbert.com

Community sites
» **Blur**: www.blursight.com

Ten Steps to Making It Work

» Change can be viewed as a cycle, and increasingly a continuous one.
» At its heart, change involves people.
» A key issue is always to ask why people should change – what's in it for them?
» Understanding their perspectives and agendas is crucial.
» It is important to understand the barriers to change.
» Similarly, it is important to understand the levers for change.
» Planning and thinking things through is crucial.
» The campaign launch phase is very important in gaining and building momentum.
» There is a key requirement to define measures for change.
» The most difficult part of any change is embedding and institutionalizing the change.

"Whether you believe you can do a thing or not, you are right."
Henry Ford

This final chapter provides a simple and effective 10-step framework for making organizational change (OC) work, irrespective of your role, the change, or the circumstances. The steps are based on the life cycle of a change program, starting at the beginning of a typical change and working to the end of its change program. Nowadays this process is a continuous cycle. The steps have been broken down into those involved in the planning of a change (steps 1-7), and those taken during the change itself (steps 8-10).

An appropriate health warning here – change is *not* a linear process. Although the steps are presented linearly, it is typical when planning a change to go through a number of iterations. The fact is that they are all connected and inter-related. Realistically you'll probably find yourselves doing all 10 in parallel! Such is the joy and fascination with a subject like OC.

Let's assume that the start point is an idea for a change that you would like to happen in your organization – a very common scenario that we've all experienced.

1. DEFINE *WHO*: ALWAYS HAVE INDIVIDUALS AT THE HEART OF YOUR CHANGE PLAN

This is the first and most important phase. The term "organizational change" has a rather depersonalized ring to it, but at the heart of any change has to be people. Change arises only from people doing things differently. The challenge then becomes one of influencing people, with their differing perspectives, insights, aspirations, views, and opinions. In planning the change, you need to take into account the main groups of stakeholders:

» The leaders and sponsors of the change are those people responsible and accountable for it. This group more than any other should have the skills, capabilities, and experience to drive the project.
» The program managers and staff are the people responsible in one way or another for managing the change. They include program staff, project staff, users, and consultants.

» Commonly referred to as the "targets", those people having to change some aspects of their work, skills, or structure, as a result of the planned change are on the receiving end of it.
» The group of people with an interest, view or position on any aspect of the change, or who can influence it, could include almost anyone to some degree.

Each of these groups can have a major impact on the change. Whatever your role within the change, whether it be leading, managing, or as a so-called target, you should take a number of actions:

» List the people involved or implicated.
» Categorize or segment them in as many ways as possible.
» Understand the relationships they have with other groups.
» Walk in their shoes. Understand their points of view, profile them, understand their drivers and motivators, determine where they are coming from.
» Seek to establish what their goals and aims are and what pressures they are under.
» Predict the possible winners and losers.
» Understand the "hats" they wear - this relates primarily to the roles they have.
» Understand their unique characters and personalities, ideally at an individual level.

In order to understand the implications for the stakeholder groups, you should review the results of this step throughout the whole life cycle of the project, which here means after every step.

2. DEFINE *WHAT* AND *WHY*: SET THE BROAD DIRECTION, INCLUDING THE RATIONALE AND ITS IMPORTANCE

The second stage builds on the first and focuses on two elements: the "what" and the "why" of the change. There is a strong causal link between these two factors so that they are inextricably linked. Generally the root driver for change is either:

» the Burning Platform type: current pain, issues, or problems (why) - with solutions (what); or

» the Compelling Vision type: future opportunity or vision (why) – with actions (what).

Each type has its advantages and disadvantages. Change agents have to define at the beginning the broad direction in which they want to go and the rationale for it, including the expected value and benefits. Given the power of the status quo and the typical powers restraining change, defining the what and the why are key levers in gaining commitment for the proposed change. It cannot be emphasized enough how important it is to focus on the question "Why change?", as you need to sell and promote the value and benefits of the proposed change.

Emphasis here is on a high-level direction, rather than a great level of detail. A famous quote from the economist John Maynard Keynes suggests, "It is better to be roughly right than precisely wrong". There are many benefits to taking this approach:

» at this stage the detail is unimportant, and will probably not be known;
» if an initiative is defeated, invariably it is not because of its overall direction but because of some aspect of the detail;
» focusing on the high level ensures that the ensuing debate occurs at the right level; and
» not having the detail at the beginning enables other key stakeholders to contribute actively and usefully in later phases of the change, thereby also creating a feeling of being consulted and involved.

It is important not to focus at this stage on where the organization is today, but on the proposed "perfect future state." The detail of the change is defined in later steps.

A sub-step here is to go back to the stakeholder analysis and assess what implications there are for each of the stakeholder groups, and what their reactions to it might be. Step into their shoes and ask, "How would I view the what and why if I were them?". Remember to do this at an individual level as much as possible.

3. UNDERSTAND THE BARRIERS, RISKS, AND ISSUES

So, having defined what the future state might look like, and the real value of attempting to get there, it's now time to get a little more pragmatic. In the heat of defining a new direction for an organization, those involved can often lose sight of all the challenges, barriers, issues, and factors that could inhibit or halt the change. A clear understanding of the barriers to change and their causes is vital for any OC. There are many, many potential barriers and risks to any change, usually far more than are in support of it. The only question is (adopting Lewin's force field technique), "Are the drivers and levers *for* change greater than those resisting it?". Figure 10.1 illustrates a typical force field analysis. The center vertical line represents today's status quo. The left-hand side represents the forces supporting the change, and the right-hand side those resisting it.

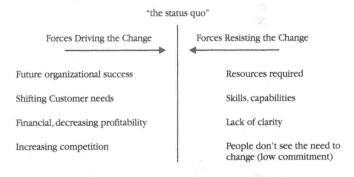

Fig. 10.1   An analysis of the forces for and against a change.

What is important here is an analysis and assessment of the types of force, and the respective power of their sources. It is also an interesting exercise to make such an analysis for the individuals and groups involved. You can then start to plan how these forces could be changed, either strengthened or weakened.

There are two other activities that you could do here:

1 assess the causes of the forces you have outlined; and
2 check and validate your assessment with other stakeholders.

As further components of this step, list the issues and risks. Now go back to step 1 and review these results from the perspective of each of the main stakeholders.

4. IDENTIFY ALL THE LEVERS, INFLUENCES, POWER, AND RESOURCES AT YOUR DISPOSAL

At this point you may feel worried, depressed, and possibly like giving up. *Don't*. Now switch to creative mode, considering all the potential levers and influences that are at your disposal. Some may not be obvious at first. Remember that change is largely a political process. The levers of change vary enormously. In trying to gain commitment, acceptance, and buy-in to a change, key levers can be:

» resources:
  » money, budget;
  » people - knowledge, commitment, motivation, skills, experience, credibility, ideas; and
  » information - education, training, communication, presentations, workshops, marketing, publicity, articles;
» formal power;
» symbols;
» promoting and publicizing successes and early or quick wins;
» new staff - management, users etc., possibly from other organizations;
» involvement and participation of all stakeholder groups;
» use of external consultants;
» emphasizing the new, interesting, and different aspects of the change;
» senior management leadership and support - visible and invisible;
» champions, evangelists, early adopters, people who have been there already; and
» incentives - financial ones and others such as promotion.

There is also a range of more coercive levers, but these may be better left to others.

Just remember the old saying, "Different strokes for different folks". Your role as change agent is to maximize as many of these resources and influences as possible.

Lastly, remember communication as a lever - don't underestimate the power and importance of communication. People impacted by or involved in the change need to have a very good awareness and understanding of the why, what, how, and when. Return to the stakeholder group analysis in step 1. It is very important that you customize communications as much as possible in order to meet every individual circumstance, need, and expectation.

5. PLAN THE CAMPAIGN – *WHAT* AND *HOW*

This step and the next form a two-step process for detailed planning. The topic that the current step addresses is how to make the first moves towards achieving the change. Fundamental questions that need to be answered include whom you will see first, what you will say, and what action you will want them to take. Your strategy here is to find a sponsor, obtain resources, and gain support for your idea and proposal. Once again the issue is one of stakeholder groups and their views on the proposals. There is only so much second-guessing you can do in the planning stage. The only way to find out the reality is to go and ask!

There are a number of questions you should ask yourself when devising your campaign:

» Do you aim high or low in the organization to begin with?
» Do you announce a high-profile launch, or adopt a more softly-softly approach?
» Do you directly tell people your ideas and what you want them to do, or first discreetly sound people out and get their reactions?

The approach you choose will depend upon the context and details of the proposed change. Golden rules for success include never giving up - persistence is crucial. Ideas and good PR are crucial, too. Use every opportunity to promote the change, seek input, and ask for support.

One of the critical elements is getting people's attention focused on your ideas. Inevitably there will be many other competing agenda items, both those related to managing the business today and those involving planning for future changes. Your case is strengthened if it addresses customer or financial issues. These more than any others get the attention of senior executives.

At this stage important questions will be asked about resourcing, benefits, alignment, and integration with other projects. This leads us to the next step - thinking things through.

6. PLAN THE *HOW*: THINK THINGS THROUGH AS MUCH AS POSSIBLE

This stage relates to the detailed planning of the campaign. It has been included because it is such an important step, and one that is rarely conducted in enough depth. It primarily involves considering the cause and effect of actions, particularly both the intended and the potential unintended consequences. It is absolutely critical that early on, here in the planning phase before any actions have been taken, you invest time in assessing the change journey and discussing fully the optimal route. With all these decisions and judgements, there is never just one right answer.

» Understand the dependencies and linkages between the various elements of the change.
» Agree which aspects of the change and its process are fixed or given, and which have a degree of flexibility – for example, job roles or the change path.
» Consider the political aspects of decisions and actions, and the potential responses and reactions that might take place.
» List any assumptions or sacred cows that are likely to be relevant.
» Define and plan contingencies.
» Create a plan to manage and minimize the risks.
» Anticipate the unexpected consequences, prepare for many eventualities, and discuss the what-ifs.
» Understand the main influences and influencers, and how they might impact others.

7. LAUNCH PHASE: BE FLEXIBLE, ADAPT, STAY COOL, PERSIST, AND DON'T GIVE UP

So, after six steps of thinking, planning, analyzing, and assessing, it's now time to press the GO button. You have the plan of action, you have the contingencies and fall-back plans. Now it's time to act. In theory this is just a matter of working through the campaign plan. Unfortunately, life just isn't like that. Things may well start to go wrong for a variety of reasons – the people you expected to have most to gain and therefore to be on your side immediately raise questions, pose problems, delay, stall, procrastinate. The project does not appear to be as high a priority as you might have hoped.

Inevitably there will be unexpected barriers and issues. You may well have planned for most of these eventualities. But you may also find there are surprise advocates and champions who rush to your aid.

The trick here is to be flexible and listen to people's advice and feedback. Work to address the barriers creatively – look for different spins that help your arguments. Keep on going back to your supporters, allies, and sponsors, looking for assistance. Don't be sidetracked into sequential activities; try lots of different things at the same time. Focus on the levers for change and the benefits to individuals.

This initial launch phase is the acid test. If your change program survives this hurdle then you're away. You need all your street-fighting skills here. Define your key messages for the stakeholders.

» What's is in for me?
» Why is it important?
» What problems or issues does it resolve?
» What value does it offer and to whom?

A point to remember is that organizational inertia is always a factor. The implication of this is that individuals and the team must face a long haul to get the issue to the position that they want it to hold.

Another point to remember is the importance of understanding others' perspectives – go back to the stakeholder analysis. Look for other routes and channels either to get to the key influencers or to get your messages heard by them.

8. DEFINE CLEAR MEASURES AND PUT MEASUREMENT SYSTEMS IN PLACE TO TRACK PROGRESS

The old adage "What gets measured, gets done" is key. OC has suffered from the poor use of objective measurements and data to track and assess the progress of change. Tracking the progress of programs and projects has historically been done with project management tools such as Gantt charts, PERT (Program Evaluation and Review Techniques) analysis, and CPA (Critical Path Analysis). All these tools rely on a relatively simple, linear assessment of deliverables. One of the major differences between project management and OC is the emphasis or focus. For OC the focus is primarily on the people and organizational aspects. Hence the aspects that need to be measured are different from those for orthodox project management.

So, having defined the scope and goals of the programs and projects, you also define appropriate measures and make an investment in collecting and reporting the data. Some of the metrics that should be applied to any change are based around the perceptions of the people involved. So it could be useful to collect data on some of the following areas:

» the percentage of those people involved who know of the program;
» the percentage who understand the goals, rationale, and purpose of the program;
» the percentage who buy into the goals and value of the change;
» the percentage who believe they will be impacted positively by the program;
» the percentage who believe they will be impacted negatively by the program;
» the percentage who know and understand their role and involvement in the program;
» the percentage who are fully committed to the program's success; and
» the percentage who know how they can put ideas into the program and give feedback on it.

Information on matters like these will prove invaluable in gauging the perception, issues, and therefore success of the program - even if the data collected is subjective.

9. SUSTAIN, INSTITUTIONALIZE, AND EMBED THE CHANGE

The most difficult piece of OC is the final bit, the last lap that focuses on embedding and internalizing the change - making it stick. In terms of the 80-20 rule, this is where the most value is derived from all that investment of resources, time, energy, and commitment. It is also the most risky area, where all the investment can be wasted.

Organizations, just like people, are resistant to change. They find it difficult, they don't have the required discipline, and they get bored and distracted easily. Lewin's three-step model of "un-freeze, change, re-freeze" captures this point. How do you lock the organization and its people into the desired "to be" state, and prevent it from slipping back into the old model?

The size of the problem depends on the type of change. With the example of a new IT system, the change is focused on new skills, new knowledge, and probably new processes. These are matters that touch only the periphery of a person's make-up and yet can be painful experiences.

But take another example – that of a fundamental culture change in an organization, such as the transition from being a technology-orientated company to being a customer-orientated one. Of course, the tangible results from this change are measured by new customers and the increase in revenues. However, the fundamental enabler or barrier is the set of human qualities. Imagine the challenge in achieving this change – one that is focused right at the heart of people's beliefs, attitudes, norms, and ways of doing things.

Changing these sorts of issues take huge amounts of time, energy, and commitment, with the risk that reverting back to the old ways is at times easy and natural to do. Momentum is easily lost after the initial impetus, glamor, and profile of the change has died away. You need to offer constant re-enforcement, using all the levers that you used in the implementation phase. There are no simple guides here. Persistence, support, leadership, communication, and incentives are the obvious levers.

10. CHANGE IS A JOURNEY – SO END, REVIEW, AND START AGAIN

The final step is both an end and a new beginning. It is an important step for all programs, not just for the minority that actually complete, but maybe more importantly for the majority that fall by the wayside during the process. Usually these are never formally closed, but die a slow, lingering death. Endings are important not only for the organization and the actual change programs, but also for the participants. Kubhler-Ross defines five stages of grief following a loss: denial, anger, bargaining, depression, and acceptance. Leaders of change programs generally never take their teams and the stakeholders through any form of closure phase. This, however, is an important component of the process, which allows various things to happen.

» Some form of celebration and reward ceremony can be held to mark the ending.
» A review or post-mortem can examine the learning points that came out of the change process. These can then be passed on to other staff, a true example of organizational learning.
» An assessment can be made of what else needs to be done. Are there new change programs or initiatives that could be launched on the back of the old one? After all, change is the only constant, and the ending of one thing signifies the beginning of something else, both for the organization and for its members.

Change, as with an organization, is an ongoing story. As the saying goes: it is not the arrival that counts, but the journey. So, go for it, enjoy it, learn from it, and then do it all over again.

"To infinity and beyond", as Buzz Lightyear would say ...

Frequently Asked Questions (FAQs)

Q1: What is organizational change (OC)?
A: See Chapters 1, 2, 3, and 6-10.

Q2: What roles exist in OC?
A: See Chapters 2, 6, 7, 9, and 10.

Q3: What processes are involved in OC?
A: See Chapters 6, 7, 9, and 10.

Q4: How do you plan for change?
A: See Chapters 6-10.

Q5: What is the leading-edge thinking in OC?
A: See Chapters 6, 8, and 9.

Q6: How does OC relate to strategy?
A: See Chapters 2, 4, and 5-9.

Q7: What are the main barriers to change?

A: See Chapters 6–10.

Q8: Who are the big names in OC?

A: See Chapters 3, 6, 8, and 9.

Q9: How do you initiate change in an organization?

A: See Chapters 6, 7, 9, and 10.

Q10: Where should I start in planning an OC?

A: See Chapters 9 and 10.

Index